A Commentary on
THE LETTERS OF JOHN

UNLOCKING THE NEW TESTAMENT

A Commentary on
THE LETTERS
OF JOHN

David Pawson

Anchor Recordings

First published in Great Britain in 2015 by
Anchor Recordings Ltd
72 The Street, Kennington, Ashford TN24 9HS

**For more of David Pawson's teaching,
including DVDs and CDs, go to
www.davidpawson.com**

**FOR FREE DOWNLOADS
www.davidpawson.org**

**For further information, email
info@davidpawsonministry.com**

ISBN 978-1-909886-69-8

Printed by Lightning Source

BEFORE YOU READ ON

In the following pages are reproduced the pages of a booklet printed for the congregation when these messages were first preached. They give a detailed overview of John's first letter. Readers are encouraged to read the whole letter with this outline in mind *before* moving on to the chapters of fuller exposition.

STUDY OUTLINE OF 1 JOHN

INTRODUCTION

1. WHO? (2:12-14)

Children	– have forgiveness.
	– have fatherhood.
Young men	– developed strength.
	– digested scripture.
	– defeated Satan.
Fathers	– length of their experience.
	– depth of their experience.
Note:	spiritual age groups rather than physical.
	church old enough to become settled, and secular.
	this epistle is for Christians only.

2. WHY? That they may be:
Satisfied (1:4) – "full".
Sinless (2:1) – the gospel for believers.
Safe (2:26) – not from persecution, but perversion.
Sure (5:13) – not intellectually or emotionally, but morally.

3. WHAT? Music rather than logic, with variations on a theme
To experience rather than expound
"Recall to Fundamentals"
Two hemispheres described:

THE WORD

THE WORLD

Church gathering at equator rather than pole.
Attractive brochures for the south; 'tourism' increasing.
Epistle is call to live in the north.

OUTLINE
LIFE (1:1–4) LIGHT (1:5–2:11)
LUST, LIES AND LAWLESSNESS (2:15–3:10)
LOVE (3:11–4:21) LIFE (5:1–21)

THE LETTERS OF JOHN

1. LIFE (1:1–4)

THE FACT OF JESUS: Two fundamentals of Christianity –
His Incarnation (1:1–2)   His Intercession (2:1–2)

A. DEMONSTRATED
The Word was   visible (lit. "gazed upon")
                    audible (lit. "listened to")
                    tangible (lit. "tested by touch")

B. DECLARED
          Essential to have first-hand witnesses.
          But John one of last apostles.
          Marks change from oral to written testimony.

C. DOUBTED
          Two worlds meet – seen and unseen.
                              temporal and eternal.
                              material and spiritual.
                              human and Divine.
                              natural and supernatural.
          Easy to believe in former.
          Possible to believe in both, if separated.
          But that both are one – in a person!!!
                    Then, GNOSTICS doubted the human in Christ.
                    Now, AGNOSTICS doubt the Divine.

THE FELLOWSHIP OF JOY:
Both horizontal and vertical cf. the two great commandments.

A. WITH OUR FATHER
          All religion aims at communion with God.
          Only Christianity bridges the gulf – from his side.
                    Can't by-pass the BRIDGE – his Son.
                    Can't by-pass the BARRIER – our sin (see 1:5–10).

B. WITH OUR BRETHREN
          Fellowship is much more than friendship.
          PARTNERS   – e.g. joint share-holders.
          PARTAKERS   – e.g. Siamese, using same blood stream.

This is "new", third dimension of Christianity (John 13:34).

2. LIGHT (1:5–2:11)

Important fact is not God's existence, but his character.
Contrast in this section between light and darkness.
But what does **"light"** refer to in God?
    a. His GLORY? i.e. dazzling beauty.
    b. His GRACE? i.e. shining on others.
    c. His GOODNESS? i.e. moral rather than physical concept.
Epistle concentrates on the third, so:
"Darkness" is evil, spiritual dirt.

PROFESSION AND PRACTICE (1:6–10)
Contrast is between "If we say..." and "If we do..."
Lip is not life. Three false professions mentioned:
    a. To be INTIMATE with God, which damages others.
    b. To be INCORRUPT like God, which deceives ourselves.
    c. To be INNOCENT before God, which denies him.
True practice will:
    a. APPLY THE LIGHT – going where it shines.
      Result: fellowship and cleansing.
    b. ADMIT THE DARKNESS – letting the light show us up.
      Result: forgiveness and cleansing.
This said to stop us sinning. N.B. accidentally, occasionally.
But if we do not conquer sin, it is still covered.

ADVOCATE AND ATONEMENT (2:1–2)
a. Jesus is our PRIEST, our PLEADER.
    a. Counsel for the defence, **qualified by** his 'righteousness'.
b. Jesus is our PROPITIATION, our PLEA.
    Atonement does not mean at-one-ment or appeasement.
    Essentially the reconciling of justice and mercy.
    Quantitative – sufficient for whole world.

LAW AND LOVE (2:3–11)
First mention of assurance – not feelings, but facts.
"Know" is experimental, personal word.
    a. The OLD commandment, to love the Father.
      Grace brings gratitude; gratitude brings goodness.
    b. The NEW commandment, to love the brother.
      This developed more fully in chs 3 and 4.

3. LUST, LIES AND LAWLESSNESS (2:18–3:10)

Note frequent use of "abide" = stay where you are.
This is a picture of "gross darkness" shown up by the light.

LUST (2:15–17)
World of sinners God loves; world of sin he hates.
a. CONTENT of worldliness. Not places or pursuits.
But where our heart is.
   i. Passion – gratification of one's appetites.
   ii. Possessiveness – greed (affluent: acquisitive!).
   iii. Pride – glory for one's self.
Compare with   Genesis 3 (woman tempted).
   Matthew 4 (Seed of woman tempted).
b. CONDEMNATION of worldliness.
i. Not of the Father.
ii. Not of the future.

LIES (2:18–28)
Wrong doctrines as dangerous as wrong desires.
End of world was imminent (not the same as immediate).
a. ANTI-CHRIST
He is being revealed, just as Christ is by his servants.
Uses perversion ("anti" can mean "instead of").
   i. They divide the church.
   Invariably leave and form an exclusive body.
   ii. They deny the Christ.
   cf. Christological heresies in the sects.
b. ANTIDOTE
Two things will keep their faith firm:
   i. Instruction (the scriptures).
   ii. Intuition (the Spirit)
At end of history both Christ and Antichrist will be seen.
We shall be ashamed if we have not stayed with Christ.

LAWLESSNESS (2:29–3:10)
Danger here is wrong association, leading to antinomianism.
Christian also needs assurance about where others stand.
The world cannot recognise a Christian (as it did not Christ).
But we can and ought to – by their character. Are they:
a. REBELLIOUS?
   i. The devil, who has –
   ii Disobedient children.
"lawless" means against, not without, the law of God.

b. RIGHTEOUS?

    i. The Son of God (note his purity and purpose).

    ii. The sons of God, who are obedient because of:

    Their HOPE (v. 2–3) – sharing his glory.

    Their HOME (v. 6) – abiding in him.

    Their HEREDITY (v. 9–10) – spiritual pregnancy.

Note on latter: these verses have led to perfectionism, pessimism.

    But: refers to **all** Christians.

            talks of **actual**, not ideal.

            tense is continuous present (i.e. habitual practice).

4. LOVE (3:11–4:21)

Peak of epistle (cf. 1 Corinthians 13).

"Brother" = fellow-Christian (cf. John 13:34).

This love is not sexual, sentimental, selective or selfish.

HUMAN RELATIONS (3:11–24)

A. The ATTITUDE of love (v. 11–15). Opposite of hate. cf. Cain.

    i. How does hate work? By seeking to destroy. i.e. MURDER.

    ii. Why does hate work? Evil dislikes goodness. i.e. MALICE.

B. The ACTIVITY of love (v. 16–18). Now example of Christ.

    i. Sacrifice–to climax of self-murder.

    ii. Sympathy – humdrum rather than heroic.

    iii. Sincerity – truth is something we **do**.

C. The ASSURANCE of love (v. 19–24)

Not based on feelings, but facts.

Hearts can give constraint or confidence, but unreliable.

Real basis is: FRUIT of love ... external fact.

            ROOT of love ... internal fact.

    Yet even this cannot by-pass simple test of obedience.

    Two commandments – believe and love.

DIVINE RELATIONS (4:1–21). Note the whole Trinity.

A. The INTOLERANCE of love (v. 1–6)

    Tolerance neither scriptural word nor Christian virtue.

    False prophets revealed because they:

        Attract the world.

        Attack the Word.

    But Christ stronger than Antichrist; truth will triumph

The VERITY of faith (v. 11–21)

"True" means "genuine" as opposed to unreal.
Our faith is a reality because of:

> i. The RECORD.
> ii. The RESULTS.
>> Four times "know" now used,
>> and each time refers to our experience.
>
> Our petitions are heard.
> Note on v. 16:
> If "death" is physical, refers to sin of ABUSE
> (cf. 1 Corinthians 11:30).
> If "death" is spiritual, refers to sin of APOSTASY
> (cf. Hebrews 6:6).
>
> Our nature is changed.
> Our kinship is Divine.
> Our understanding is true.

Contents

This book is based on a series of talks. Originating as it does from the spoken word, its style will be found by many readers to be somewhat different from my usual written style. It is hoped that this will not detract from the substance of the biblical teaching found here.

As always, I ask the reader to compare everything I say or write with what is written in the Bible and, if at any point a conflict is found, always to rely upon the clear teaching of scripture.

David Pawson

THE WORD OF LIFE

Read 1 John 1:1–4

Tucked away in the back of the New Testament are these three little letters given the titles in our Bibles: 1, 2 and 3 John. From earliest times these letters, even though they didn't have a name attached to them, have been attributed to the apostle John. When one compares their grammar and vocabulary with that in the Gospel of John there is no doubt that they come from the same pen.

Here is a mature man. Of all the disciples, one was allowed by God to live to a ripe old age – the apostle John, the beloved apostle, the one closest to Jesus. He moved from the Holy Land to Ephesus in his latter years. There this old man would exhort the Christians in the churches of Asia Minor to stay true to the Christ whom he had known. So these letters (and indeed the Gospel of John) were written when he was the last apostle still alive to remember the Lord Jesus and he can say, "We touched him, we saw him, we listened to his voice." It must have been wonderful to have one man in your church who had actually known Jesus in the flesh. Of course we have no-one who knew him like that, though we can know him just as well. Nevertheless, it is interesting to read the writings of a man who walked with him on the dusty lanes of Galilee.

Why did John write these letters? The answer is in 1 John 5:13, "I write this to you who believe in the name of the Son of God that you may know that you have eternal life." It is possible to *believe* without *knowing*. You may still have doubts, you may still be a bit uncertain. Even after you have begun to believe in Jesus you might say, "I wonder if I am a real Christian? Sometimes I feel like I don't really have the life that he promised me." There may be that uncertainty and doubt even in a believer's life. It is God's will that a believer should *know*, should be absolutely certain, so that if anybody stops you and asks "Are you a Christian?" you would not say "I hope so" or "I'm trying to be" or "I'd like to think I am." You would say, "Yes, I am." You would be certain. You would know, not because you thought you were better than anyone else, nor because you were boasting, but because you know that you have eternal life.

God does not want us to be left in doubt. A Christian in doubt is not much use to himself or others because their testimony would be hesitant when people ask them about Christ. But if you know that you have eternal life, as well as saying "I believe" you can say "I know whom I have believed." Then you are that much further along in the Christian life. Do come with me through these letters of John so that you may know that you believe, and make sure that you have real life, eternal life.

This is vital to Christians for a number of reasons. Your joy cannot be complete unless you know. Joy is related to certainty. Only if you are absolutely sure of Christ can you be joyful. Your holiness is related to certainty. You can only live a holy life if you are sure of Christ. Your fellowship is related to your certainty. If you are not sure of eternal life then you cannot have full fellowship with other Christians or with God. So John is writing that they may be sure. This is relevant today because there has even crept into church terminology an expression which to me is a contradiction in terms: "Christian agnostic".

A person who had walked with a fellowship I led many years ago wrote to me and said, "I am now a Christian agnostic." A famous preacher in London published a book with that title. It has become fashionable to say you can be a Christian and almost boast that you are not sure – that you are one of the "don't knows"; that you call yourself a Christian but you are not quite sure about many things in the Bible, about Jesus Christ, about eternal life, about life after death. But to say you are a "Christian agnostic" is to say you are a square circle. A Christian is meant to know. We are not meant to offer apologies to the world, we are not meant to go to the world and say "I'm not really sure". We are meant to proclaim a ringing assurance, a certain testimony. We know whom we have believed.

How do we know? John is going to give them certain tests of how you may discover if you or anyone else is a real, true Christian. If you have real life, how do you test the genuine thing? How do you know when you really have got the true faith? There are four tests. I will give certain technical names for them and then explain them. There is a *historical* test of true faith, there is a *theological* test, there is a *moral* test, and there is a *social* test. By these tests, which you can apply to yourself, to a preacher or to anybody claiming to be a Christian, you can discern the counterfeit from the genuine.

First of all there are the *historical* tests of your faith. Is your faith based on facts rather than feelings, on things that actually happened rather than on things that you feel and experience, fancies of the mind, fictions of other people? Christianity is unique. It is an historical religion. Its book, its sacred scriptures are therefore full of history. If you compare the Bible with the Koran or any other scriptures of different religions you discover that they are books of ideas whereas the Bible is a book of historical fact.

So is your faith based on fact, not feeling? That is the first thing. The mystics' faith is based on feeling. The Christian faith is based on things which actually happened. It is true because they actually happened. "That which we have seen, that which we heard, that which we touched...." My faith is in something that could be seen and touched and therefore it is a true and sure faith and you can't shake it. Mind you, if my faith were based on my mystical experience – my feelings – then I would be a Christian every Sunday night and I wouldn't be one every Monday morning. My feelings go up and down like yours – of course they do.

If my faith is going to be based on my experience then it is shaky from the start, but if it is going to be true and real it is based on the events of history, and supremely that event of Jesus which split history into two. He actually did walk the earth and people actually touched him, they actually saw him with real eyes, heard him with real ears. My faith is based on history. If someone could prove that Jesus never lived or never died, or that he never rose again, then my faith would collapse. No-one has ever been able to prove that, although they have tried. Books have been published and some people have even prepared books for publication and then cancelled and rewritten them because the evidence convinced them of the facts. So that is the first test of real Christianity: is your Christian faith based on the facts? Because, if it is, the facts will not change and therefore your faith will be sure.

The second test is the *theological* test – what you believe. "What think you of Christ?" is this test. If you have a right view of Christ, then you have a genuine Christian life. What does this mean? It means to believe that Jesus was both human and divine together; that Jesus was God become man; that he wasn't just the greatest man or the greatest mystic or the greatest healer or teacher that there has ever been, but that he was God and that he was a real man.

Now if people outside the church find it difficult to believe he was God, people inside the church find it difficult to believe that he was and is man, but he is still man today. He is a human being and still divine. "There is only one mediator between God and man, the man Christ Jesus." When we pray to Jesus we are praying to a human being – that is why we don't need to pray through a human priest, Jesus is a human priest. That is why we don't need to pray to Mary, feeling that she may be more human and understand – *he* is human and he understands. We go straight to this human being who is a divine being as well. To believe that Jesus Christ is the Son of God come in the flesh—that is the theological test.

However highly someone thinks of Jesus, if they do not believe that, then it is not genuine Christianity. They may have a tremendous admiration for him as Gandhi had, as Tolstoy had, as Dostoevsky had. They wrote about Jesus as the greatest teacher there ever was, and the way to live is to copy him, but they didn't believe he was God. So it is not genuine – that is not Christianity.

The third test is the *moral* test – a person who has really found Christianity (which means really has found Christ) has a moral change in their life and they do not live the same as they did. In other words, it leads to a changed life with new standards. It leads to a life that keeps the commandments of God. That is a very simple test. If you do not keep the commandments of God, if you live the same life you used to, then your Christianity is counterfeit. It is not the real thing, not true.

The fourth test is the *social* test—if a man says he loves God and he doesn't love his fellow Christian, he doesn't love God. If you really find Christ then you love Christians. A person who doesn't get along with other Christians is not a Christian. A person who doesn't love his brothers and sisters in Christ doesn't love Christ. They may say they do, they may have their name on a church membership roll, they may have been through all the rites and ceremonies, but it is not genuine Christianity. If we don't love one another then don't let's kid ourselves or anyone else that we are loving God.

Now these are the four tests of genuine Christianity, which the apostle John is wanting us to apply. He is asking whether your faith is historical (based on the facts of Jesus); is your faith theological (have you got a right view of Jesus as divine and human?); is your faith moral (has it led to a change in life, and has it led you to keep the commandments of God?); is your faith a social faith (does it lead you to love Christians, or to keep yourself to yourself?) That fourth one is the most acid test of all.

There is a story told of the apostle John in his old age. He got so old that he had to be carried. The younger Christian men in Ephesus used to carry him in their arms into church every Sunday. He would be called upon to address the company from his chair. He would say just one sentence in an old, quivery voice: "Little children, love one another." It is all he would say. You know what it is like when an older member of the church always says the same thing in prayer or anything else. The younger people get a bit restless and say, "Same old thing."

I remember an old man in a prayer meeting who always used to say, "Lord, sweep the cobwebs from my heart," until finally one young man got so sick of the phrase he got up and say, "Lord, kill that spider!" Apparently some of the younger people in the church of Ephesus asked John why he always said the one thing that they were tired of hearing. John replied, "Because it is the Lord's command." If only this is done it is enough, and that will be the emphasis in this epistle. It is in this short letter that we have the matchless statement "God is love". You won't find it anywhere else in the Bible. Whoever loves is born of God and knows God.

It is interesting that the word "know" comes twenty-five times in this letter – "that you may know" – and as we read it we must judge ourselves. Not only will the four tests tell you who are the genuine Christians and who really does belong to Christ, it will also reveal, as John says, that some of those who were once members of the church are members of the church no longer because they were proved not to be real Christians. They went out because they were not of us.

The tests in 1 John also reveal who are the counterfeit ones who have made a profession of faith that is not genuine faith. You can't read this letter without getting the impression that John is attacking people. He is calling them false prophets, deceivers, antichrists – strong labels. Why is he doing this? Because the greatest danger to the church is not persecution from outside but perversion from inside – people who twist and distort Christianity until it is no longer genuine, even if it carries the label. Can we identify the group of people whom John has in mind as he attacks them in this letter? Yes, I think we can. There was a group of people in the early days of the church called "Gnostics". Now if an agnostic is someone who says "I don't know", a gnostic is someone who says "I do know". In fact the word means "know-all." There was a group of people called "know-alls" and they said, "We know everything, we know all the answers to the human questions." They were not a Christian group originally, they were a pagan group. They talked about having an enlightened mind, and they were living very freely in their morals because they said, "We're enlightened. We're not old fashioned, we're not narrow-minded like our parents and grandparents. We have free beliefs and we have free behaviour." So they lived a free life and invited others to join them. They practised meditation and mysticism. They practised religion, but they lived quite freely. Some of them became ascetic and denied themselves food and sex and sleep, but most of them went the opposite way, over-indulging themselves.

These people began to get into the church. They began to say, "We will show you a better way." You can still call it Christianity but we will enlighten your mind. You can be free from all the old taboos that the old Christians used to have. They didn't like to do this and didn't like to do that, but we are enlightened and we will enlighten you. This was devilish stuff. Now there were two things that they taught: one concerned belief and one concerned behaviour. I mention them because in fact Gnosticism is creeping back in.

It was a mixture in those days of Western intellectualism and Eastern mysticism, and was almost identical to the kind of thinking that lies behind so much that was happening to some of the young generation from the 1970s onwards. I used to see in young people's rooms pictures stuck on the walls of Indian mysticism alongside their scientific textbooks on the shelf – the same kind of "enlightened" loose-living that was characteristic of this Gnosticism.

What was the belief of the Gnostics? They believed that matter is fundamentally evil; that anything physical is evil and impure, therefore – and this is the point – they said God would never become a physical being; God would never become matter down here. Therefore, the man Jesus, while being a great man, they thought was not born of a virgin and was no more than a great man doing his own thing. That is precisely what many today are saying. They may think Jesus was a great man doing his own thing, expressing himself, but they don't believe more than that.

The Gnostics said God couldn't have become man so they had the weirdest explanation of Jesus. They said *Jesus* was a man but the *Christ* was a kind of spirit who came upon Jesus after his baptism and left him before the cross, but that Jesus stayed a man. Now this is just twisting the facts until you can't recognise them, and the result showed in their life.

If you believe that matter is essentially evil (as the Christian Scientists and theosophists do), sooner or later you will come to one of two extremes in behaviour. You either become so ascetic that you starve yourself and whip yourself and do things to yourself that harm you, or you indulge yourself and say, "The way I live doesn't affect my religious life. I keep my religion to the spirit and what I do with my flesh doesn't affect it."

One of the disturbing things in our day is that we get people who think they can be Christians and can go on living the way they did before, who don't realise you can't keep fellowship with Christ unless you let go of the life that you have lived before, the life that indulged self, the life that was lived around self, the life that simply said, "Oh, it doesn't matter." It does matter, and in the case of a person who will not change their life and who doesn't let Christ change their life, their Christianity will last a matter of weeks because it isn't the real thing. It hasn't gone deep enough; it is a form of Gnosticism.

There is another story told about the aged apostle John. One day he went to the Roman bathhouses in Ephesus for a bath. He got in the water and suddenly he rushed out of the water, pulled his robe around him, and ran out of the baths. Why? Because he spotted someone at the other end of the pool, a man called Cerinthus. We know from history that Cerinthus was a leader of the Gnostic heresy, the man who was damaging the faith of Christians, and John said, "Let us fly lest even the bathhouse fall down because Cerinthus the enemy of faith is within." Today John would be regarded as an eccentric. In this age of tolerance when we put up with almost anything, the idea of a man getting out of a swimming pool because there was a man in it who believed this kind of rubbish – this would be said to be intolerant, eccentric, even just a little bit mad.

Where are the Christians today who will say, "I will have nothing to do with a man who teaches that, I will have nothing to do with false teaching, I will have nothing to do with a man who twists Christianity." Today the call is, "Let's sit down and have dialogue with him," but John the apostle's message is let's get out of here, we don't even want to talk to a man who twists things like that.

He will say it in his second letter in which he writes: If anyone doesn't come to you with true doctrine, don't welcome him. It's poison. It's dangerous. The call today is for people like the apostle John who will attack the counterfeit religion of our day and say: you may have your mysticism, you can say you have religion, you can say you've met God, but you haven't come within a million miles of meeting him. That is not real, it is not true, it is not genuine because it didn't meet the God and Father of Jesus Christ.

It is against such a background that this letter was written. We will see that John says that if someone denies the reality of sin in their life, they deceive themselves. Denying that Jesus is God come in the flesh is also deception. The truth is that genuine Christianity is historical, based on facts. It is theological – it believes the right thing about Jesus. It is moral – it leads to a new life. It is social – it leads to loving one another.

The key phrase in 1 John 1 is at the end of v. 1, "The word of life". *Preaching the gospel is preaching the word of life*. The funny thing is that everybody is wanting life, real life. Why are people taking drugs? Why are people so anxious to go places and do things? Because they want to live, because they want real life. What is real life? First of all it is a greater *quantity* of life than most people enjoy. Secondly, it is a greater *quality* of life.

First of all, a greater *quantity*. Don't you feel that life is desperately short? Older people find it is rushing by so fast now you wonder how you can put the brakes on. The years have gone so quickly and they go with an increasing rush. Life is brief. It was never meant to be. Our human desires and dreams need a much longer life than 70 to 90 years, and the word of life tells you that you can have much more than that. You can have everlasting life. You never need to say goodbye. Isn't that good news?

Secondly, the word of life says that the life will be of greater *quality*, it will be eternal. Living this life forever would be misery. I remember Fred Hoyle, a professor of astronomy, saying, "I would like to live three hundred years but no more." Well if his life were all that he had I would not blame him for saying that would be enough. But when you discover real love, don't you want to live forever? Some of the most solemn words said in a marriage service are "Until death do us part". If you really love someone, that is a ghastly phrase and you want to say: I need everlasting life to go on loving as I really do now.

The "word of life" offers you a life of a quantity adequate to fulfil your deepest dreams, and a quality deep enough to satisfy. It is a longer life than you would otherwise know and it is a deeper life than you would otherwise know. How do we get this life? The answer is life of this quantity and quality resides in God. He is everlasting, he is eternal, he has life in quantity and quality. But how do I get it? There is a gulf between me and God – I just have a limited time span and I just exist here. He is in heaven. He is Spirit – I can't see him, I can't touch him and I can't hear him. He is beyond me, so how do I get this life? The answer is in the fact of Jesus. That which was from the beginning, the life of God, became the life of man and that life was touched and seen and heard.

You see the message? The eternal has become the historical in Jesus. The life that was God's life has become man's life in Jesus. It all came down to earth – life came, life was manifested in him. Life was seen in him – you could look at Jesus and you could say, "Now that's life. It's life in quality, it's also life in quantity because he lived before his birth and he lived after his death." That is life.

Anybody who really studies the life of Jesus comes to the conclusion: now this is life. This is life as it was really meant to be lived. When they discover that he existed from all time, before he was born, and that he will exist to all time after he died, then they say, "Now this is life – quantity and quality." Jesus said, "I am the life." So it starts with the fact of Jesus, the divine manifestation of life, and then the human message passing it on.

This was how God decided to give us life—to manifest that life in Jesus within human life, and then to get a group of people who saw it, heard it, touched it, to pass it on and to say what we have seen we know, proclaim and declare to you. Right down through the ages this message has been passed on: that if you want life, you come to Jesus for it. Those who knew him in the flesh, those who knew him down here on earth, said, "This is life." He said, "I have come that you might have life, and that you might have it more abundantly." Quantity, quality – yours.

What is the result of getting this life? A fellowship of joy. "Why?" John says, "... that you may have fellowship with us." Now this word "fellowship" is so abused. It is used of human friendship but it means more than that. I am reminded of the Shetland Islands where I began my ministry, where many of the men in the congregation were fishermen, great big burly chaps with their navy blue polo neck sweaters, coming into church straight from a night's fishing. Five or six of the men would bunch together and buy a boat, maybe for ten thousand pounds, and they were partners in the boat. If it sank they all suffered. It was their boat, none of them could take part of it out, they shared it. In the New Testament they would have been said to have "fellowship" in the boat. In other words, nobody could contract out of it.

The boat was shared. This is what fellowship means. It was used in the Greek language of Siamese twins with the same bloodstream going through them both. They had fellowship in blood – neither could live without the other. "Fellowship," said John, "that we have is fellowship with the Father and with Jesus." All of us are sharing Christ's life together, and wherever the word of life is preached and accepted there is created a fellowship of joy as people know real life. "This is life eternal to know you, and Jesus Christ whom you have sent," says Jesus in his prayer.

John says, "I'm writing all this to you so that your joy may be complete, that you may be filled with joy." Pleasure is delight in things, happiness is delight in people, *joy* is delight in the Lord. Your joy is not complete until you are having fellowship with the Father, with Jesus his Son, and with one another. That fellowship comes from having genuine faith, genuine Christianity, genuine life through receiving the word of life.

"GOD IS LIGHT"

Read 1 John 1:5–10

There are things in 1 John 1 which (if taken alone) are terrifying, and in v. 5 we find the most terrifying statement in the Bible: "God is light."

Many people believe in the existence of God and it doesn't seem to make that much difference to their daily lives, but what matters is what *kind* of a God you believe in. There were two men on the bridge of a ship one lovely starlit night with a calm sea and the moon floating through the clouds, and one who was a Christian said to the other, "It's easy to believe in God on a night like this." The other said, "Oh yes, I believe in a God – who is as far away as those stars and as cold as that sea." They both looked out on the same sea and each believed in quite a different kind of God.

If people are asked what kind of a God they believe in, some would start by saying "God is love." That is a popular notion of God in Britain, and indeed it is a true statement, found twice in the fourth chapter of this letter. It is the only place in the Bible where it says this. But if you only believe that God is love then that statement of itself can lead to dangerous misunderstanding, mainly for the reason that the word "love" (in the English language) means so many different things to different people. There are those who limit "love" to sex, and of course to say "God is sex" would be ridiculous. But even more dangerous is thinking of "love" in terms of *sentiment*. That perhaps is the deepest difficulty of saying "God is love" today. We have such a sentimental view of love, which is why people say, "Well, if God is love there can't be such a place as hell." Only if your "love" is sentiment would you say that. If you understand the love of God you would see there has got to be a hell.

So if you start with the statement "God is love" you are liable to misunderstand his love. Where does the Bible begin? What is the fundamental statement about the God we believe in? It is not "God is love", it is "God is light." Only when you start there can you go on to say that God is love without risk of misunderstanding. The Bible begins that way. The very first thing God made was light: "Let there be light" on the first day. All the way through the Bible you get this sense that God is blazing, dazzling, glorious light.

What does it mean to say God is light? Physically, of course, if you could see God now you would be blinded. It is a merciful providence that veils God's glory from my eyes because they couldn't stand it. Even with thick sunglasses I couldn't stand the sight of the glory of God. I shall need a new body with new eyes to gaze upon his glory. I can't even look at the midday sun without damaging my sight. God's glory leaves the midday sun looking like a little lantern. So it does refer to his physical light in a sense. When God appeared to the people in the Bible they saw brilliant light – they had to hide their faces, and hours afterwards their faces shone with reflected light, but it is more than that.

I am going to be very down to earth now because I think I can convey this best by referring you to the numerous advertisements for detergents and biological miracles. If I said "God is whiteness" I think I will convey exactly what this means: dazzling whiteness. In other words, no dirt at all. The soap manufacturers are competing to tell you that their product will get rid of every little speck of dirt out of your clothes and that they will be dazzling white. When it says "God is light" it means that in his character and in his personality there is not the slightest dirty thing at all:

dazzling white. When you understand that, you understand what the Bible means by darkness. It means foulness, dirt, filth – just the opposite of God. So: "God is light and in him is no darkness at all." There is no other person of whom you can say that. This is how the Bible starts with God. Then you realise therefore that there are problems. How can God mix with the likes of me? How can I have fellowship with God the Father and with his Son, Jesus Christ? The nearer you get to them both, the more you feel, "Depart from me, I'm a sinful man, O Lord." You are exposed by the light. Yes, so many of the soap advertisements take the dazzling whiteness of their own clothes and then they put something washed in another powder alongside, and as soon as the two come close together you can see. When God, who is dazzling whiteness, and man get anywhere near each other, the contrast is so stark.

Would you wash your clothes and get them all nice, dazzling white and clean, and then put them back in the dirty clothes basket mixed in with all the filthy things? Of course you wouldn't. You have a different container in which you put your dirty clothes. They go to be washed, they come out clean. Then where do you put them? In a clean drawer. You put them with clean clothes. You would be a fool to put them with anything else. How, then, can a God who is like that mix with the likes of me? How can there be fellowship between us? How can we have that life which is life knowing him if that is what we are like? The answer is very simple: you can only have fellowship with God on God's terms, and those terms are that you be clean.

I remember an old man who had a great gift for talking to people anywhere, anyhow, just starting a conversation and getting around to something spiritual. But he came unstuck badly with one lady he was talking to because he told her that she needed a bath before she went to heaven. She was very offended at this but he then tried to explain and he did get over the problem. He was trying to tell her that you will never get to God unless you literally come clean and, as we will see in a moment, part of coming clean is to confess. Indeed we say, "Come clean over it. Get it out. Tell him what you have done. Confess your sin." You'll never get to God unless you come clean.

In v. 6 John draws the conclusion that if a person claims to know God and lives a dirty life then, frankly, he is a living lie. The truth is not in him. He is deceiving himself and he is deceiving other people. This is a test: someone who claims to know a holy God and who lives in sin is just not telling the truth. It can't be real and it can't be true. John is getting at those who were coming in and saying, "Spiritual and physical things are two different things; you can have mystical experiences of God and it doesn't matter how you live." But it does matter. If you go on living in darkness then you can't know the God of light.

Anyone who thinks they can play around with God and with sin will find very quickly that they cannot do it. God is light, and if we walk in darkness we cannot know light. The one thing that is absolutely true is this: light and darkness cannot coexist. You cannot have light and darkness in the same room. If you have light, it's light. If you have darkness, it's darkness.

We had darkness at a service in a church where I ministered – pitch blackness. Somebody had a torch, and when they shone that torch the light overcame the darkness, and where the torch shone there was no darkness. If God is in your life there can be no darkness. If your life is dark then God can't be in it.

But on the positive side: if we walk in the light as he is in the light.... Notice that your standard of light must not be keeping up with the people next door but as *he* is in the light. You are to walk after God as he walks. Wherever he shines, you say, "That's the way I'm going to take." Wherever he throws light on your path and says, "This is the right thing" – if you go that way then I will tell you two things that will happen. First of all you will have fellowship with other Christians. We have fellowship with one another, which means that if I walk in darkness I cut myself off from Christian fellowship. What is it that divides Christians from each other? Sin. That is the only thing that ever divided Christians. If people who belong to a God of light walk in darkness, they can't have fellowship with one another.

The other thing that happens is this: *the blood of Jesus goes on cleansing me*. Literally, the tense of the verb means that the blood of Jesus goes on cleansing me every day. If I am walking in the light, I am not perfect but I am heading for perfection. If I am walking in the light I am not claiming to have got rid of all the darkness but I am claiming to be in the position where the blood of Jesus can keep cleansing. In other words, we are not being told here that you must be perfect before you can walk with the God of light, what you do need is to continue that walk, which means a steady progress in the right direction in the path that God lights up for you. Then you will find that every day the blood of Jesus goes on cleansing and keeping you clean. There will be dirt to clean but the blood of Jesus will clean it up. That is the first thing John has to say.

It is quite amazing how people hate the word "sin" as soon as you mention it. People outside the church don't like it, and alas some people inside the church don't like it. I remember hearing a lady going home after a service (I had not been the preacher). I had been in the pew and overheard the remark: "Oh, he's on about sin again"– as if this is the one thing you mustn't get on to. But look at this epistle! The word "sin" comes once in v. 7, once in v. 8, twice in

v. 9, once in v. 10, once in v. 1 of the next chapter, twice in v. 2 of the next chapter – and this is written to Christians, believers, that they may know that they have eternal life. You will not only believe in Jesus by facing the little word "sin", you will have life by facing up to it.

What does this word "sin" mean? It is not the same as the word "vice" and it is not the same as the word "crime". Vice is something I do against myself. Crime is something I do against someone else. Sin is what I do against God. I may have no vices, I may have committed no crimes, but that does not mean I am not a sinner. Again, just as the word "love" has got too tied up with sex, the words "vice" and "sin" and "crime" have too. The phrase "living in sin" has become so narrow in its meaning that if I said that "so and so is living in sin" you would probably jump to a wrong conclusion. To live in sin is to live in temper, in jealousy, in impatience, in worry. Let's stop the world giving narrow meanings to these things and say that to live in sin is to live out of God. To live in sin is to live without love. That is what sin is.

Sin is not only what we *do*; it is what we *are*. Think of that story I mentioned earlier about the cobwebs and the spider – the old man praying every week, "Lord, sweep the cobwebs from my heart" and the young person getting sick of it and saying, "Lord kill that spider." Now if I can use this: the cobwebs are the sins we do, the spider is the sin we are. If we could get rid of all the sins that we do, we would still find that sin would be there. It is not just that I have done wrong things, it is that I *am* wrong or, as it is expressed here, it is not just that I have sinned, it is that I have sin. There's something wrong with me. I try to keep the commandments and I break them. Why? Because there is something wrong with me.

These two facts of what we *do* and what we *are* have been denied by many. There was a day when I would have denied them. I would have denied them hotly as a young student, and if anybody had said "You are a sinner" I would have denied it straightaway. Let's look at the denials in v. 8. It is full of "ifs" here, and you notice how personal John makes it, "If we...." Let's not think about other people! "If we say we have no sin, we deceive ourselves and the truth is not in us." Now here is the basic question: do you believe that your nature is really good or really bad? Stripping away all your upbringing and everything else, stripping away the social veneer, getting really down to you, are you a bad guy or a good guy? There is only one true answer to that: I am bad! That is the only true self-estimate. You will come one day to the realisation that a great saint called Paul came to: "In me [that is in my flesh], there dwells no good thing." You have got to be a pretty mature Christian before you believe that. But they who would serve God best are "conscious most of wrong within". The nearer you get to God the less you feel about yourself and the more you see yourself as you really are. One great saint used to say, "Lord Jesus, you took me from behind my back where I had hidden myself and you set me there before my face and, lo, I am ugly with sin."

The greater the saint the worse they feel they are. They have come to the truth. If a man says, "I just do a few bad things but I'm really good; if you really knew me, I'm a good chap", that man has deceived himself and it is the worst kind of deception there is, because who is going to get you out of it? To fool others is one thing, but to fool yourself! How will you ever get out of that? You are living in a dream world, out of touch with reality.

Anyone who thinks he is good has never faced the truth. If we say we have no sin, if we say that our nature isn't evil and perverted, then we deceive ourselves. We don't usually fool many other people, I notice, especially those we live with. If I started saying to you "I have no sin" you could very easily check up with my wife and family. Then you would say, "You're fooling yourself but you haven't fooled another single soul – you deceive yourself."

The other denial is: "If we say we have not sinned...." If someone denies what he *is*, he deceives himself and if he denies what he *does* then he makes God a liar. How could anyone deny this? Surely nobody would ever stand up and say "I have not sinned." Oh yes, people do! I did. How do you say this? How do you deny that you have sinned? First by saying that you are not responsible for what you did, that it was fate not your fault; that it was your heredity, "Well, my grandfather did this and it's in the blood you know." Or it's my environment: "If you'd been brought up as I was you would do the same." This is so often now a plea in court.

We are getting to the stage where people do not believe that we are responsible for our own actions. We are victims or patients. "Sin is a disease, not a rebellion...." Yet the Bible states utterly clearly that every one of us is held responsible by God for what we do. So who is right? Are we all simply victims (as suggested in behaviourist psychology)? Are we all simply a bundle of complexes and cannot help doing what we do? Or are we rebels declaring independence of God and saying, "I'll do this whether you tell me it is wrong or not." God says that you are responsible for what you do. Don't care what anybody else says. If I say I am not responsible then I call God a liar; if I say that I couldn't help doing wrong, I call him a liar.

The second way in which people deny that they have sinned is to say that it is not terrible. "Well, everybody has their faults but it's harmless; it's just weakness, it's just the failure of human nature. Don't call it sin, it's just weakness."

Yet a third way is the extraordinary form of perfectionism in which some people get to the point where they say "I am incapable of sinning." That is an even more incredible state.

I have met some people who thought like that. But according to 1 John – and again we remind ourselves that he is writing to Christians – if we say we have not sinned then it's your word against God's. He says you have, you say you haven't. He says all have sinned and come short of the glory of God; you say you are the exception. Who is the liar? You or God?

If you say that God is the liar then his word is not in us. What does that mean? Someone who says, "I have not sinned" is not putting this Word in his heart. A person who says "I have not sinned" never reads his Bible. I find that the more I read the Bible the worse I feel. I feel like Pilgrim in *The Pilgrim's Progress* – as he read the Bible the burden on his back gets bigger and bigger. You realise that it is true, that John's readers behaved in the way you behaved, and they were called sinners for it, and so are you.

Take the Sermon on the Mount – John says the message we had from Jesus was that God is light. I have heard people say that Jesus came to bring us the message that "God is love", and that is partly true. But the message which John the beloved apostle gave, the message which we have heard from him and declare to you, is that God is light. Where did Jesus say that? Right through the Sermon on the Mount. What is the theme of the Sermon on the Mount? God is light; he demands that we should be poor in spirit and pure in heart, and meek. He tells us that murder, adultery, lying and other things are not only deeds but thoughts, and this concerns what we are inside as well as what we are outside. He demands that we never think of revenge, and that we turn the other cheek when we are hurt; that we never think of our rights or our reputation; that we never swear, and that we are faithful to our partners for our whole lives. As you read through the Sermon on the Mount, the searchlight of God's light shines on your life. I have never met anyone who could read the Sermon on the Mount and say "I've lived up to that." If a man says "I have not sinned" then this Word is not in him. He hasn't read it; he hasn't studied it.

But now look at the lovely verse (v. 9) that comes in between two denials of having sinned. This is the most beautiful verse in 1 John, and if this verse were not there it would all be terrifying: "If we confess our sins, he is faithful and just to forgive ... and to cleanse...." Millions of people, I believe, have come to that verse and found hope and joy, and found that they could get through to a God of light. It does not mean you come perfect, but confess; if you come clean to a clean God then he will accept you. To come clean is to be quite specific. Many Roman Catholics are a good deal better at confession than many Protestants. We do not have to confess to a priest, but at least many of them confess their sins before they go to mass. We should not come to communion before we have "come clean". Jesus said that if you have a gift, before you bring it to the altar go and get something right with your brother before you come. Confession is to be specific. "If we confess our sins...." Notice the little "s" at the end. It is easy to say we are all miserable sinners and we confess our sin – but to confess our sins means, "I'm sorry I said that to so and so yesterday; I'm sorry I was cross with the children when I shouldn't have been; I'm sorry I brought home that paper from the office, it wasn't mine."

General Booth confessed his sins and became a Christian because of a pencil in his pocket which he had stolen from another boy. He said, "Lord, I confess that the pencil in my pocket is not mine."

If you confess particular sins and come clean about it, what kind of a reception will you get? Sometimes I have spoken to someone and said, "Why don't you tell God that you've done wrong?" They don't quite know how God will take it, so they don't know whether to come. But God is faithful.

He has promised that if you come, and come clean, he will meet you more than halfway.

Susanna Wesley, the mother of John and Charles Wesley, was a great woman. As soon as her children were old enough to understand, she said, "Now look children, if ever you do something that you know to be wrong and you come and tell me that you have done it, I will never punish you. But if I find out that you have done something wrong before you tell me, I will punish you severely." She was a wise mother and one could wish that every parent would say that to their children. God has made similar promises: If you'll come and tell me first, I will not punish. If you'll confess your sins, I'll keep my word, I'll be faithful. But just a moment—it says, "I will not only be faithful but I will be just." How can God be just if I come and say, "Lord I've done something wrong" and he lets me off? How is that just? This is why the cross is central to all forgiveness. Every act of forgiveness is written in the blood of Jesus. Why? Because he was punished for our sins. God will not demand punishment twice if we confess. He will be faithful to his word and he will be just, and because our Lord Jesus has already paid the penalty for that sin he will wipe it out as if it has never been. He will forgive, and there is nothing like forgiveness to bring fellowship with God. Nobody has such fellowship with God as the person who has been deeply and wonderfully forgiven.

Do you remember the woman who came and washed Jesus' feet with her hair? She disgraced herself in public but Jesus said: she loves me much because much has been forgiven. Maybe we don't have more fellowship with God because we don't confess our sins enough. We don't come and claim this promise. But there is something more. Not only does he forgive sins but he cleanses us. Sin is a debt to be remitted, it is a stain to be removed, and every time I have sinned there is a stain left in my character. There is a stain left in my personality. What can wash away my stain? Nothing but the blood of Jesus, cleansing from all unrighteousness.

David, after he had sinned terribly against God and against a fellow man, after he had done that to Bathsheba and to Uriah, came to God and confessed it. In matchless words in Psalm 51 he said, "If you will wash me, I will be whiter than snow". You will never see anything whiter than snow on this earth. If you hang up your dazzling white washing next time the snow has just fallen, it will look dirty. God will not only remit the debt of sin – for that has been paid by Jesus – he will cleanse the stain of unrighteousness.

What is John saying in this letter? Real Christianity must be based on truth. Real Christianity must be based on facts. First of all, historical facts. In vv. 1–4 that which was seen and heard and touched – real happenings. But second, it must be based on personal facts, personal truths. To summarise, there is the truth about God in three aspects—and you must face that truth if you want fellowship with God. He is light, he is dazzling white; he is clean, there is no dirt in him at all—face that truth. Face, secondly, the truth that you are sin and that you have done sins. Face up to that and come and say, "God be merciful to me, a sinner." Thirdly, face up to the truth of Jesus – that he died for your sins. If you only had the truth about God and the truth about yourself, you would be further away than ever before. The gulf would be too deep and too wide ever to cross and you would never come to God and you would never know him. But the truth about Jesus is that he bridged that gulf in two ways: first by stepping from the divine into the human, and second by being made sin for us – do you see how he did it? Jesus brought the life of God, the word of life, all the way from glory to earth, to be made a curse and to die that we might have life and fellowship and joy, and live with the God of light. Such is the message of this book: a terrible message;

a serious message. If God is like that, he is a terrible God to the sinner. But if God is the God who sent his Son to die and to shed his blood that I might come, then he is a wonderful God, and this is a wonderful passage.

"I AM WRITING"

Read 1 John 2:1–14

Sometimes people ask me, "How do you begin to study a passage of scripture? How do you start to get the truth out of it and understand it?" I can only speak for myself. I don't pull out a great pile of commentaries and start reading what everybody else says about it. I start with the Bible and I read the passage and I read the passage again, and do so repeatedly. This is the first step—you will never get any truth out of the Bible if you just read it once and say, "Well, that's my bit for today done, I've read my passage," and then simply read notes or comments on it. If you are really going to read the Bible you must read the same passage over and over again.

The second thing I do is to look for a word or phrase that comes up more than once in the passage and is something that begins to stand out. As soon as I see that, I get a coloured pen and underline it. If more than one word comes out, one gets underlined in red, another in green and so on. Certain words and phrases begin to shine out as features of the passage.

In 1 John 2:1–14 there is one phrase that appears nine times. I wonder if you noticed it. Maybe you would have to read it two or three more times before you notice. The key phrase is "I am writing". What is the significance of this? We recall that this is one of the few letters in the New Testament that has no name and address at the beginning. It doesn't say "John the apostle to the saints who are at Ephesus." There is no author name, no address for the letter to go to. Putting together these two facts – that there is no name and address, and that the author keeps saying "I am writing; I write", what do we assume? There is one simple explanation: the man who wrote this letter was writing to people he knew well, and who knew him well, and he was actually with them when he wrote. In other words, he could have said all this to them but he was going to write it down for them. So he is saying: I'm writing this for particular reasons; I could have spoken to you, but I am writing this. I have written this to you young men; I have written to you little children; I am writing this for particular reasons. When I was pastor of a church I would write to the members in a monthly newsletter. Of course they could talk to me at other times too. But normally I was saying something in the letter that I wanted to write down so it could be read more than once. If I say something to you, I can only say it once and then it is over – the sermon is preached (unless you get a recording of it later). But if I write something down, then you can pick it up and read it, pause and think about something in it, so that you don't have to rush on. Reading this letter of John you can stop at any point and think about it. Sometimes church members have said to me, "I wish I could stop you in the middle of a sermon and ask you questions," or, "I wish I could just stop and think about that." John is writing so that his readers can think about it and really meditate on it.

Incidentally, this is one great advantage of preaching through the Bible. The sermon is delivered once and then it is finished, but you can take your Bible home. You can read it, you can stop anywhere you wish and think about it. After hearing a Bible passage in church it is good to spend time reflecting on it at home. "I am writing to you," says John. He could have preached, he could have said it to the church, but he was writing it. We can thank God that he did, because we don't have a single sermon of the apostle John! There were none of the electronic gadgets that are such a help to us today. They managed without them quite well! This means that every sermon John preached is lost – but when he wrote it for them, that has come down through the centuries and it is now the Word of God to us. Thank God that his Word comes to us, not just spoken from the mouth but written in a book. Christianity will always remain the religion of a book because these people of God wrote. So this letter is like the pastor's letter in the newssheet of the church at Ephesus, from John writing sixty years after Christ died, and still what he saw and heard and touched is alive.

John has special reasons for putting it down in writing. In 1:4 he writes, "We are writing this that Your joy may be complete." Did you ever see writing a letter as a means of completing joy? Can you imagine writing a letter to complete someone's joy? That would be a lovely thing to do.

John says in 5:13, "I write this to you who believe in the name of the Son of God, that you may know that you have eternal life." There is another reason for writing a letter to Christians: to help them to have confidence – to be sure. There could be someone, a Christian somewhere in the world who is going through a period of doubt and uncertainty and they are wondering if they are a Christian. Could you write a letter to them, that they may know, to help them to be sure?

There are many other reasons for writing. The first one stated in this passage is this, "I am writing this to you so that you may not sin." There could be someone, perhaps a young person away from home, who is facing temptation, and a letter from you could just stop them sinning. You could write to them and say, "I feel that you may be going through a time of doubt and uncertainty, or that you may be having pressures put upon you. I would like you to know that I am praying that you will not fall and that you'll keep true to what you know to be right." Somebody far away could be kept from sinning because you wrote.

Behind 2:1–6 lie two basic understandings: (1) God is King, therefore he governs; so he has the right to make laws and to give commands. He sits on a throne and he is the lawgiver, the great commander. (2) To sin is to break his laws, to rebel against his commands and say, "I'm not having you telling me what to do – I will do what I want." John is teaching: I am writing all this down so that you will not break the commandments of God. That is what the first part of this chapter is about. These two facts are not altered one bit when you become a Christian. There is a false understanding around: that when you are a Christian you are finished with the commandments of God; that you are no longer under law but under grace so that now you can do what you like. The most dangerous sentence I have ever heard was coined sixteen hundred years ago: "Love God and do what you like." That is not a sentence from the Bible. It is not true that if you love God you can do what you like. What is true is this: Love God and do what *he* likes. That is what the Bible teaches. In other words, you weren't saved *from* keeping the commandments you were saved *for* keeping the commandments. You weren't saved to throw God's laws out of the window; you were saved to live by them. John was writing so that believers may not sin.

Perhaps I could put it this way: the normal Christian does not sin. Now that is a really startling statement but it is going to pop up again in chapter three and in chapter five. The normal Christian does not sin but the average Christian does sin. Do you know the difference? If you are sinning as a Christian then you are an average Christian but you are not a normal Christian. Let me go a little further than that: God's desire is not only to forgive your sin, but to set you free from it.

Do you know the most challenging thing someone ever said to me? They looked me straight in the face and said,

"Tell me one sin that Jesus has saved you from." If you are asked what Jesus has saved you from, it would be true to say, "He saved me from the penalty of sin; he saved me from hell; he saved me from death." All that is true. But what sins has he saved you from? What did there used to be in your life that is no longer there? Temper? Jealousy? Impatience? Self-centredness? Pride? What has gone?

"Little children, I am writing to you so that you may not sin." In other words, the normal Christian life is to get rid of sin. Why does John say this? Because he has been saying that if we sin, we just need to confess and it is cleansed. Somebody could easily say, "Oh well, that's fine. Now I can do what I want. Now I can sin any time I like. I can just come every night and get it all clean." That is a terrible misunderstanding. It is God's intention that we should not sin, not that we should go on having to come for forgiveness. It is his intention not only to forgive sin but to get rid of it and to set us free from it.

Therefore a complacency that says "now I'm a Christian I can do what I like – I can sin and it doesn't really matter because I can get cleansed and forgiven" is a misunderstanding of the gospel. The trouble is that as soon as we deal with that extreme of complacency, people switch over to the other extreme of despair and say, "Well, if the normal Christian life is sinless then frankly I haven't even begun. I still sin. I still do wrong. So you are ruling me right out as a Christian."

John now begins to pick up those who despair. He is saying that if anyone does sin we have got everything that we need to cover that situation. It is walking the narrow line between the complacency that says, "Sin doesn't matter, not now," and the despair that says, "I've sinned so I'm not even a Christian." Both these extremes are to be avoided. To those who think it doesn't matter how you live now that you are a Christian, John is saying: I am writing to you that you may not sin. To those who are in despair because they have sinned as a Christian, John is saying that if anyone sins you have got someone to pick you up again. Let me underline: *those who are in despair*. I don't know which group you are in; I hope neither. But it may be I am directing this to someone who has sinned as a Christian and who feels that this has undone the good that Jesus has done in their life, that they have gone down, and they are depressed. Listen to what John says: you have an advocate, and you have an atonement. Even if you do fall as a Christian, remember this.

What does it mean that you have an advocate? It means having counsel for the defence in court, the best lawyer to defend you, somebody who will stand for you. You have Jesus, the human Jesus, Jesus Christ the divine; you have Jesus Christ the righteous – the fairest, best person who ever lived. So when you come into God's presence and you hang your head in shame because of what you have done, somebody there starts speaking for you. You have the best defence you could possibly have. We have an advocate, somebody who goes straight to God and can say, "I am pleading for David Pawson" (or whoever it is).

Now if he is a righteous advocate, what can he plead? Can he plead that there were extenuating circumstances? "He was under pressure?" Can he plead for me that I am basically innocent and that it wasn't sin? No, he can't. But I remember once sitting in a court of law and hearing the counsel for the defence say to the judge, "I am not claiming this person is innocent, but I am pleading with you on this ground: he has suffered enough already as punishment for this crime." Will Jesus Christ the righteous plead on those grounds for us? No, but I can tell you what he will say: "I have suffered enough for the punishment of this sin." That is a plea that God, the holy Judge, accepts. God then says:

acquitted, dealt with.

Here are the two extremes again. There are those who think it doesn't matter if you sin after you are a Christian, and those who think it matters too much; those who think that because God forgives you can break the commandments and get away with it and it doesn't really matter, and those who think, "I have sinned, therefore I have lost my salvation." Neither of these is the true Christian path, which is to say, "God has called me not to sin, and I press after that. But, if I do sin on the way, I go straight to my counsel for the defence and ask him to plead." Isn't that a lovely balance? It saves you from complacency and from despair. It saves you from getting proud of yourself, saves you from getting too ground down by your failure. Forgetting the things that are behind and stretching forward to the things that are before, you press on toward the high calling of God in Christ Jesus. This is the balance.

So the first thing John is saying here is that the Christian life is to be a life that is empty of disobedience to the commands of God. The commands of God, on the positive side, are to be kept. This unmentionable four-letter word "duty" again. It doesn't come in here, but the idea does. We are called to duty – to keep the commandments of God. Life is not just a life that is empty of sin, but it is full of obedience; not just a life that is free from disobedience but a life that is useful. I have met a number of people who thought that a good life was a life that was free from evil. "I never did anybody any harm in my life" - that kind of statement, as if that makes you a good person. But the Bible makes it quite clear that a good life is not just one that is harmless but one that is fruitful; not just empty of bad things but full of good things. Frankly, there is no-one so miserable or so off-putting as a person who is empty of all bad things and hasn't got anything good in them. They are like a house swept clean and worse spirits come back into it.

One of the tests of whether we know God is this: you cannot possibly know God if you are breaking his commandments. You cannot possibly say, "I know God" if it is patently obvious that you break his laws. There is a logic here, so let me take you through the steps of the logic. If you know God, you love him. You can't help but love him if you know him. If you don't know him you don't love him, but if you know God you love him. You are bound to, he is such a lovely person. Everybody who gets to know God loves him, so if you know him you love him. Step number two in the logic: if you love him you keep his commandments. Says the young boy to the young girl, "Your wish is my command." Says the believer to his heavenly Father, "Your command is my wish." If you love him, you want to do what he wants. Love God and do what *he* likes, and if you really do love God you will *want* to do what he likes. Jesus said, "If you love me, you will keep my commandments."

Now that is the logic: if you know God you love him, if you love God you keep his commandments; therefore, if you keep his commandments that is proof that you know God. Someone who doesn't keep his commandments may shout from the housetops "I know God" but it is a lie. He may say "I love God" but it is a lie. You cannot love God and not keep his commandments. These two things go together. When Jesus said, "Love God with all your heart, soul, mind, and strength," he was saying, "Keep the commandments."

You can run through them: "Have no other gods before me, no graven images, reverence my name and hallow it, keep the Sabbath day, honour your father and mother, don't kill, don't commit adultery, don't steal, don't bear false witness, don't covet." Here is the proof that you love God, and it is as simple as that. It is a proof that we don't love God, a proof that we don't know him very well, if we break his commandments. If we know him, we love him; if we love him we keep his commandments; if we keep his commandments it is proof that we know him.

John is all the time in this letter dealing with a very unfortunate, tragic feature of church life in those days and today: that there are people who profess to be Christians who are not. There are people who say they know God who do not. There are people who say they love God and they do not. There are people who say they have not sinned and they lie, and the truth is not in them. Recall, in 1:6, "If we say we have fellowship with him while we walk in darkness..." and in v. 8, "If we say we have no sin we deceive ourselves", and in v. 10, "If we say we have not sinned...." Now in 2:6, "He who says he abides in him", and in 2:9, "He who says he is in the light...." What you say with your lips is not very convincing unless your life shows it. Therefore, it behoves us to not accept any Christian on profession of faith. Let me underline that. We must not accept a person as a Christian because they *say* they are. Plenty of people say they know God. Who is it who knows God? He who loves him. Who loves him? He who keeps his commandments. Who is it who knows God? He who says he is a sinner. Who is it who really does know God? He who walks in the light and loves his brother. In other words, if my lips say one thing and my life says another, I'm a living lie, I'm not a Christian at all and I shouldn't go around saying that I am. John is concerned to weed out of the church those who *say* but do not *do*.

He mentions two particular professions here in 2:4 and 2:6. He has already mentioned those who say "I know him", but he mentions in v. 6 those who say they *abide* in Christ. Therefore if a man says this, he must walk as Christ walked. You must be able to look at his life and say that is how Christ would have behaved, what Christ would have done, what Christ would have said and how Christ would have reacted.

Now let me underline 2:5, "Whoever keeps his word, in him truly love for God is perfected".

I read a history of England in the 1950s and 1960s entitled *The Neophiliacs*. It was a shattering book. There arose a new way of thinking called the "new morality" which said something like this: all we need is love, and that we need no laws, no commandments, no authority, just love. This bred a new generation that honestly believed that love and law are incompatible, that they don't belong together, and that the answer to our world's problems was to get rid of all the laws and just have love. But this is nonsense. Love and law belong inextricably together. You cannot have one without the other, and to love someone is to keep their laws. People became so frustrated, they want love and they see that it doesn't solve the world's problems. This leads to violence and misunderstanding, it drives generations away from each other. The more they shouted in that era "Make love", the less love there seemed to be and the more limited it was. Let me tell you what real love is. Real love is to keep commandments – that is all. If you love God you accept his laws for your life, and then you know what real love is. So that "new morality" which arose from the 1960s taught quite wrongly (and quite unbiblically) that provided we have got "love" we don't need laws, and that provided two people love each other sincerely you don't need any laws on their sexual behaviour or anything else. This is a contradiction in terms. You can't love and do what you like, you must love and do what God likes.

Therefore, what we desperately need is the kind of love that is law-abiding – that's love. It says "law-abiding" – "If his commandments abide in you." In other words, a loving person is a law-abiding person, and that is the proof of their love. A Christian is a law-abiding citizen, not just to the laws of God but to the laws of men too, and that is taught in the

New Testament. Breakdown of law and order is due to the fact that love has been divorced from law. Can you see what is happening? Love and law are partners; righteousness and peace kiss each other, and love is loyalty.

Here is an illustration. Many people today decide because they love each other to live together. They say, "What does it matter that we get legally married? It is only a legal ceremony. We love each other truly, we are going to live together and that's it," and they do. But real love says, "There is a law of marriage." Furthermore, real love is prepared to make certain promises because real love is *loyalty* and therefore real love means saying together, "I promise to have and to hold from this day forward, for better for worse, for richer for poorer, in sickness and in health...." This is the law of marriage, and love is accepting the law of marriage, "till death us do part".

Many marriages are breaking up because love is being divorced from law. A man says, "Well now I love someone else, so love tells me to go to her," but that is not true love. Love accepts the law and loyalty of marriage.

This is what John is saying: If you really love God, you keep his laws. Love is loyalty; love abides in the law and the law abides in the person.

We move on to 2:7–11. John now speaks even more tenderly. He has called his readers "my little children" and now he calls them "brothers". That word almost sounds artificial now because there is such a lack of love. When a pompous minister gets up and says, "Dearly beloved brethren..." people think it doesn't mean a thing. But it is a lovely word.

Here John is saying: Brethren, I want to tell you of one of the special commandments we have as Christians. It is "Love one another."

"A new commandment I give to you," said Jesus, "that

you love one another." John is now going to make the point that the proof of loving Christ is that you love Christians. A man who says "I love Christ" and doesn't love his fellow Christians is a liar. As we have already seen, such a person is not telling the truth. You cannot love Christ and stay away from Christians. You may profess to, but it can't be done.

John is looking back to the day when he was busy fishing in the Sea of Galilee near the seashore and Jesus came along and said "Follow me". He also said that to James. I am not sure how James and John got on with each other – I suspect badly, they were called the "Sons of Thunder". I can guess there were a few eruptions in that family. Jesus was inviting the disciples to join him, but they would all have to live with the others. You cannot follow Christ as a private individual. Some Christians try, and they say, "Well, I'm just going to have my private devotions." But if you love Christ you love Christians. If you hate them, you hate him. If you dislike them, you dislike him. If you do it to them, you do it to him, because inasmuch as you do it to the least of these his brethren you do it to him. You cannot divorce loving Christ from loving Christians.

So this is an old commandment that goes back to the days of Jesus. John's readers have had it from the beginning of their Christian lives: you have heard it from the beginning. But John is teaching that it now comes to you in a new way because you can now see it as well as hear it; the light is already dispersing the darkness; this commandment is true in Jesus and it is true in you. What does this mean? John is saying that we know that we are to love Christians not only because we have heard it from the beginning but because we now see it in the saints.

It was noticeable some time ago that something new is happening amongst Christians. People who would never normally be in each other's houses are meeting in homes to pray, to read the Bible and to love one another. People who normally would never have crossed paths are inquiring about one another's health and welfare and are concerned about each other. A new thing is happening; you can see it as well as hear it. John teaches that if you don't like your fellow Christians you are living in the darkness. You are blind. You can't see where you're going. You lack direction; you lack a goal; you lack purpose. But if you love your fellow Christian, then you are walking in the light.

A Christian who dislikes his fellow Christians doesn't see what he is like. He doesn't see what a contradiction he is. He thinks he is still a Christian, but he is not – whereas those who really love their fellow Christians can pick their way forward without stumbling, without falling. They can see where they are going, they are in the light.

Do note that for John – and for the whole Bible – there is no middle course. You are either in the light or the darkness. You either hate your fellow Christians or you love them. You are either in the kingdom of God or in the kingdom of Satan; there is nothing in the middle. I find that modern thought is quite the opposite. In modern thinking we are all a bunch of greys: nobody is going to heaven, nobody is going to hell. We are all heading for somewhere mixed up in the middle. But the Bible says there is a radical and complete difference between the best unbeliever and the poorest Christian, something that will divide them eternally. As you look at people's lives this is not always apparent. The outside of their lives may be quite similar but there is a line right through every congregation and every community. On one side are those who are in the light, on the other side those who are in darkness. On the one side those who know and love God, on the other side those who don't know and don't love God, there is nothing in the middle. People have objected to the Bible because of this. In fact I have frequently had people say to me after a sermon: "You put things so black and white; you are so dogmatic, it is either/or." But I am just doing what John did. I am just doing what the Bible does: facing people with the fact that you can't sit on the fence. You must be living on one side or the other. You are either loving your fellow Christians or you are hating them, you can't be anything else. Now someone may say, "Well, I don't love my fellow Christians very much but I don't hate them either." That is not true because hating is not just having a feeling of dislike, it is ignoring them. Do you remember when God said, "Jacob have I loved, Esau have I hated?" What did he mean? That he disliked Esau? No, but that he ignored him. In the Bible the word "hate", like the word "love", is not so much how you feel but how you act. It is your attitude of will towards a person. If you ignore them, if you don't meet with them, if you just live as if they do not exist, you are hating them. If you serve them in their need, if you pray for them, if you seek to help them, you are loving them, whatever your feelings are. If you are "hating" them it means you are ignoring them and leaving them alone. But you can't be both, you are one or the other.

Now we move to vv. 12–14. We have thought about the commandments of the Father, which we are to keep. We have thought about the community of the Son – when you come to Jesus you come to Christians; you become part of his body and you are to love them. Now we come to the communion with God that the Holy Spirit has given us.

We have seen that Christianity is a matter of keeping the law and walking in the light, or loving your Father enough to keep the law, loving your brother, your fellow Christian, enough to walk in the light. These are the two great facets of the Christian life: loving the Father, loving the brother, keeping the laws and walking in the light.

However, it is very important to know that nobody ever

got to be a Christian by doing those things. This is the most awful misunderstanding that I must avoid. I have told you that the Christian life is keeping the Ten Commandments, but if I told you that keeping the Ten Commandments makes you a Christian then I would not be preaching the gospel. Supposing I wore an American suit and put on a ten gallon Stetson hat, smoked a cigar, talked with a Texan drawl and chewed gum, that wouldn't make me an American! I might fool some people but I am not an American! On the other hand, I suppose I could get American citizenship and become a naturalized American. Then if I were to wear an English tweed suit and talk with an Oxford accent, that wouldn't make me an Englishman. There is a radical difference between an American and an Englishman, and it is not a difference of behaviour but something much deeper. John is saying, in effect: I am writing these things to you because you are already Christians. He would not tell them to keep the commandments if they were not Christians. That would be wrong advice. It means: I am writing these things to you because you already know certain things. What do they know? He divides them up into age groups: little children; young men; fathers. Some who are reading this may be little children spiritually. Some may be young spiritually, going through the turbulent adolescence that every Christian goes through, which is part of growing up. Some will be "fathers" who have walked with the Lord a long time. I can only say to you "Keep the commandments and walk in the light" because you know certain things. What do you know? Little children, even if you are just a beginner in the Christian life, you know at least two things. You know that your sins are forgiven, not because you have kept the commandments but for the sake of Jesus Christ. "My little children, I write to you because you know your sins are forgiven for his sake." Christ died for you, and that is what is getting you to heaven. Therefore,

I can say to you now keep the commandments – not to get to heaven but because you are going there. You are to walk in the light and love your brother not because you are trying to be a Christian but because you already are one, and this is what a Christian does. You know also the Father; you can call God "Father", you are not a lost orphan in a lonely world any more, you have a Father you can talk to. You are part of a family and you can come to God the Father. Therefore, love your Father and love your brothers and sisters.

Young men, you have gone a little further in your Christian life and you know that it is a battle. You have had terrific battles with the devil in your Christian life but you have found that you can overcome the evil one. When you have let the Word of God abide in you – you are strong and you have overcome the evil one.

To fathers – if you have been a Christian many years – you know him who was from the beginning. A baby Christian just knows forgiveness and that they have a Father they can talk to. A Christian who has grown up a bit has been through battles and they discover that the Word of God can make them strong to overcome Satan, but all this is knowledge concerning evil. An older Christian who has walked with the Lord can say, "I know God; I know the Lord and he is very precious to me."

In other words, a young Christian's testimony is about what God has done *for* him or her, but an older Christian's testimony is what God *is* to him or her.

Whether your main experience is what God has done for you, or over the years what God is to you, my word to you, all ages, is this: love God with all your heart, soul, mind, and strength; perfect your love by keeping his laws, and walk in the light by loving your brother.

What is John really saying? Don't ever stop at what you are saved *from*, ask what you are being saved *for*. You are saved from breaking the commandments but you are saved for keeping the commandments. You are saved from hatred; you are saved for love. You are saved from darkness but you are saved for light.

Therefore, the Christian life is a life of loving the Father, loving the brethren, keeping the commandments and walking in the light. A person who doesn't go on to do those things is not a Christian, they have misunderstood salvation. They have professed to know him; they have professed to abide in Christ, but they do not. John is writing in order that his readers may know that they have eternal life and continue to believe in the name of the Son of God. (See 5:13.)

ABIDE

Read 1 John 2:12–27

The key word that comes up more often than others in this passage is "abide". It appears twenty-four times in the letter. People love singing "Abide with me" at football matches and on other occasions. There is something in this word "abide" that gets you. Why? It means to stay right where you are, to be fixed. To let anything *abide* in you means to let that thing stay in your heart.

The word is going right out of the English language. Why? Because few people abide anywhere for long nowadays. They are moving house, changing jobs, going from one place to another in cars, trains and aircraft. Nobody talks of abiding anywhere. If you are still living in the town in which you were born, you are an exception, an abiding exception. What is the opposite of the word "abide"? It could be "fleeting", "passing" or "passing through". To say "I've been here all my life and I shall be here for the rest of my life" would be abiding. But "I'm just here while the job brings me here" is not abiding, it is passing.

There is such a contrast between the abiding God and the passing scene of this world. That same hymn "Abide with me" has the line "Change and decay in all around I see" – everything is passing; the scene is shifting the whole time.

Today, many people love lights that move instead of lights that just shine in the same place. Abiding lights they can't abide, so they have got to flash and move all over the place and we have all got to be on the move. It is said that a tourist, jumping into a taxi in London, said, "Drive on, drive on." The taxi driver said, "Where to?" The visitor replied, "I don't care and I haven't time to think, just drive me on." I am sure that is apocryphal but it is an apt picture of the age in which we live.

The important question in life is not where you go but where you stay, not where you pass through but where you abide, where you make your home, where you settle, where you really belong, where you really say, "Now this is where I want to be and this is where I want to go on being."

John is going to plead with the people to whom he is writing – to *abide in Christ*. There are two sorts of religion that I know — there's the "abide with me" religion and there is the "abide with him" religion. Everybody wants the "abide with me" religion. They want God to look after them; they want God to stay with them, but the real religion that lasts is not so much abide with me but abide with him.

I remember again a German telling me that once in Hitler Youth, he was hauled up before a desk, and behind the desk was a German officer who said, "Where do you live?" This young man said, "I live in Stuttgart." "Wrong, where do you live?" "I live in Germany." "Wrong, where do you live?" "I live in the Third Reich." "Wrong, where do you live?" He went on pressing him like this and finally the poor boy said, "Well I don't know what answer to give." The officer said, "You live in Hitler. That's where you belong." Years later that boy found himself in a prisoner of war camp in England, and through the barbed wire a lay preacher used to push sandwiches to him in the early days of the war when it was not popular to fraternise with prisoners, and because of that simple gesture he is now a minister of the gospel, and if you ask him where he lives now he would say, "I live in Christ, that's where I live now; I'm no longer in Hitler I'm abiding in Christ. I may be anywhere in the world but I have got a fixed home. I may change my address but I've got a fixed dwelling place for all generations. I live in Christ."

The secret of the Christian life, of abiding in Christ, is saying, "This is where I'm staying. This is where I belong and nobody's going to get me out of Christ. This is where I want to live."

We begin with what I have called the "taboo of the Father". If you are going to abide in him, the first thing you have got to learn is that you must not love the world. *You cannot abide in Christ and love the world at the same time.*

Straightaway, we see a seeming contradiction in scripture. God loved the world and then told me not to love the world! Why should he love it and not me? What is the difference between God loving the world and then telling me, "Do not love the world"? The answer could be in the word "world" which means different things in different pages of the Bible. Sometimes it means the earth on which we live; sometimes it means the world of human beings, the human race; sometimes it means this godless society in which we live; sometimes it means the satanic kingdom, the system of world government which Satan heads up.

In the first two senses God loved the world—he loved the earth; he made it. He loved the human race, he made it. But he does not love the godless society or the satanic system in which we live, and nor are we to do so. Or it could be that the difference between God having loved the world and our not loving it is in the word "love". God's love only seeks to give. God loved the world because he wants to change it and make it different. When we love the world we want to be like the world. God's love wants to take sinners out of the world, whereas when we love the world we want to get right into it. So there is a difference in our love, which is why it is better to use the word "lust" for what we are talking about now, and the word "love" for the purer thing. Therefore John draws a contrast between lust and love. It is a pity that in the English language we tend to use "love" for everything from the most selfish and brutal desire to the most holy and unselfish affection. But let us keep the two words "love" and "lust" separate. We are commanded not to love either the social or material side of the world in which we live. "Love not the world or the things in the world," and there isn't one of us who will come unscathed, I think, through a reading of this passage. There are three things mentioned particularly: the lust of the flesh, the lust of the eyes and the pride of life. It is a tragedy that the world has given to those three titles a solely sexual meaning and connotation. If we let the world dictate the meaning of these three phrases, we will not feel the biting edge or the challenge of them. It includes perversion of sex but it includes far more than that. What is meant by the lust of the flesh? Let me put it this way: any appetite of the body that stretches beyond the limits that God has set for that appetite is the lust of the flesh and it can be anything.

Sex is an appetite of the body which God gave. He made sex, he made mankind male and female. But he has set a limit beyond which that appetite must not go, and the limit is marriage. Sex beyond that, either beforehand in fornication or afterwards in adultery, becomes lust because it has gone beyond the limit. Within the limit it is a good and holy thing and none of us would be here but for sex.

Let us take some other illustrations to get away from that. Consider food. Our body has been given a natural appetite for food and I enjoy my food and I hope you do. That is a sign of health. But God has set a limit, and beyond that limit people become too fond of their food or too fussy with their food. As soon as you have gone beyond the limit and live to eat instead of eating to live then you have become a glutton and it is a lust of the flesh. Sleep is a natural appetite of the body and you need an adequate amount of it. But as soon as that passes over into sloth and laziness and lying in bed when you don't need to, then it has become a lust of the flesh.

I could go on with so many things—the desire for warmth in the body can become a slavish devotion to comfort and pandering to oneself. As soon as a natural appetite goes beyond the limits that God has set and becomes an end in itself and something for which you are now living, then it is a lust of the flesh. Take the lust of the eyes – once again people have given it a narrow sexual connotation but let me give you a paraphrase: "the ambition to buy everything that appeals to you." You could walk through a shop and have the lust of the eyes all the way at every aisle. It means the desires come to you from outside you. The lust of the flesh comes from inside; the lust of the eyes comes from outside. You see something, you want it, so you try to get it. It could be a car, a house, an antique piece of furniture or anything. Let us take a biblical view of all these things.

What is the "pride of life"? If lust is what you have when you can't get a thing or when you don't have it, pride is what you have when you do get it: the person who is always boasting about how cheaply they got this, or how clever he was in buying that. In other words, having got the things you have lusted after, now you are proud of it. Here is a very simple illustration. I remember meeting a man who was wearing a polo neck jumper and I could see his muscles rippling underneath the wool. He lived for bodybuilding. It had begun as a young man with a natural desire of the flesh to be fit (a good thing). So he had been a keen sportsman, and then he had gone in for bodybuilding, and he had got a chest expander, weights, and all the rest of it. Bit by bit, this desire for physical health became an end instead of a means. He was now living to be fit instead of being fit to live, and his wife told me that it became an obsession with him. The Bible says "bodily exercise profits" but it also says "bodily exercise profits little". It is a minor thing according to Paul, and there are other things that are more important. Spiritual exercise is much more important. But the man I was referring to was now living for this, and it was the lust of the flesh as he became obsessed with a desire to be fitter than others. Then it became the lust of the eyes because he began to take a bodybuilding magazine and he saw photographs of Mr. Universe. He began to see things that he would like himself and he began to covet, and lust of the eyes is coveting – it is the same thing. So he began to say, "I want to be like these chaps in the pictures." "You too can have a body like mine" – so he tried and succeeded. The next thing was pride of life because he became a magnificent specimen and he had photographs taken and put in the magazine. The pride of life took over and these three things had come. His poor wife said she never could take him out to anything, never saw him; he was too busy building up for the next photograph or the next competition or something.

Do you see how it worked? It started with a natural desire of the flesh that God had given, that should have been kept within limits. It became a lust of the flesh, then when he saw certain things in others – lust of the eyes in that he wanted them. Then it became the pride of life, "I am going to be Mr. Universe." Now that can happen to any of us in relation to anything in the world, and we have got to watch this. Why? Before I tell you why, I would mention that when I look at the temptation of Eve in the Garden of Eden I find the same three things. There was lust of the flesh: she wanted that fruit. There was lust of the eyes: she saw that it was good; pleasing to the sight. There was pride of life: "You can be like God, have the fruit" – and she took it.

I see the three things when the devil tried it on with Jesus. A temptation is made to flesh: you are hungry, let your hunger go beyond the limits God has set; make these stones into bread. A temptation is directed to the eyes: the devil took him up on a mountain and showed him all the kingdoms of the world and said, "Look at them; wouldn't you like them?" A temptation is made which would appeal to others' pride of life. Wouldn't you like everybody to say, "Oh, look at him floating down from the pinnacle of the temple?" The devil didn't succeed with Jesus but he succeeded with others.

What is wrong with these things? I want now to be very practical and give you three simple questions that will tell you whether a thing is worldly. A Christian must not be worldly. How do you know when you are being worldly? Some people think it is just a matter of having a list of places to which you don't go. "Well, I don't go to this and I don't go to that. You won't find me in the casino or the night club, so I'm not worldly." Don't you believe it – it is not a matter of where you go. There are three questions: where does this thing come from? How is it affecting me now? Where will it lead me? John is telling us that worldliness comes from a particular place, it has a particular effect on you and it leads you in a particular direction.

The lust of the flesh, the lust of the eyes and the pride of life do not come from God. They are not of the Father, they are of the world. You didn't get it from him; you got it from someone else. I remember a lady going up to a Baptist minister and saying to him, "Now look, I want a straight answer to a straight question: Am I wrong to be smoking?" That minister simply looked at her but didn't answer, he asked her a question. He said, "Madam, is it a lust of the flesh or is it of the Spirit?" She looked at him for half a minute in silence and she said, "Thank you, that settles it," and she walked away. He was making her face up to the matter: where did this come from? Where did you get it? Nobody ever smoked a cigarette because God told them to, as far as I know. Where did you smoke first? In the bushes with those lads at school? At least that is where I smoked my first. I didn't get it from either my earthly father or my heavenly Father, I got it from the world. So I ask where something came from. Did I pick it up from God? Is it a God-given desire of my body, or is it something I picked up from someone else? That is the first question.

These things are not of the Father, John is saying. They don't come from God. It is interesting that in 2:14–16 he mentions the world, the flesh and the devil. That is where they come from. What effect does this have now? John says that you cannot love the things of the world and love the Father at the same time. The heart isn't big enough to love both. You have a limited amount of love. You can love your Father, you can love your brother, but you can't love the world at the same time. If you love the world you don't love your Father. So here is the question: doing this, do I love the Father more or less? What effect is it having on my love for God? A worldly thing will reduce my love for God. A God-given thing will increase my love for God. You can see that the same thing could be worldly to one and God-given to another. I have been in some gardens where the garden was the "god" of the person who made it. Every bit of time and energy was given to a superb garden, and it was: "My garden, look at my garden, look what I've done," and it had become the world to someone because the love for the Father was being squeezed by it. But another keen gardener says, "Look at that flower, isn't God wonderful to have made a flower like that?" A garden could be worldly to one and not to the other. So we must not go around pointing fingers and saying "That's worldly" in other people's lives; we must rather point at ourselves and say, "That is worldly for me because my love for God is less through doing it."

What does it lead to? John says, "Don't you know that the world is passing away?" It is disintegrating, and if you build your life on things of the world it is going to crash as your life and you will have nothing to show for it.

I have met some people who are now retired and have nothing to show for their lives. It is hollow. They have lived for their career, their money, their big house, and now that they have gone there is nothing. The world is passing away and the lusts of it pass away, and you have nothing to show for it.

I remember a house, a beautiful bungalow in a large city. It could have appeared on an Ideal Home magazine cover. There were huge picture windows – not, I think, to let the people who were inside get the view, but to let the people outside get the view in, because there wasn't much of a view outside. You could see inside the lavish furnishings. The owner spent every spare penny he had on it

The last time I went to that city I said, "Where's that bungalow gone? It's not there," and I was told that it was demolished to make way for a road. It was under a demolition order all that time, and the man was just pouring his life into that home and it had gone. I asked where the man was and was told: "When it was pulled down he had a heart attack and died." So he has gone. There is that man's life with nothing to show for it. It had gone. The world is passing away and the lusts of it, and for him that was a lust of the flesh and it has gone and he has gone.

The question John would ask is: where is this thing leading you? Is it leading you to build your life on things that are going, to decorate a house that is going to be demolished? Or is it going to lead you to something permanent that doesn't disintegrate?

How do we know when a thing is worldly? Where did it come from? Did it come from God? What effect is it having on my love for God now? Do I love God more because I do this or have this? Is it leading to nothing or is it building something for eternity? John is making it clear what "worldliness" is.

What is the opposite of lust? The opposite is love. "He who does the will of God abides forever." In other words, if you are lusting after the things of the world you will be finished, your days are numbered. If you are doing the will of God you abide, you stay, you remain, you are there, you are fixed, you are permanent. Why should this be? Because if I build my life on the world, the world is passing and my life will pass. But if I build my life on God – he doesn't pass, he abides and therefore my life abides. It is as simple as that. Build on the one who is going to last, and you last. Build on something that is passing and you pass.

There are thousands of people who are building on things that are passing and who will have nothing to show for their lives when it comes to the end. But those who seek to do God's will *abide*. This world is on the way out, its days are numbered, the sentence of God is upon it: it is going to be demolished. The whole world – all human science, all human commerce, all human achievement – is going to be demolished. Only one class of people will remain and abide: those who do God's will.

We have given a lot of attention to three verses but they are important. So far we have been considering the pressures because the church is in the world. Now we turn to the pressures that come because the world gets into the church, the other pressure under which a Christian has to live. He not only lives in the world outside the church, sometimes the world gets in. Now at first sight there is no connection between v. 18 and v. 17, but there is. The world is passing away and one of the signs that it is, and one of the signs that we are getting near the end of it, is that there is rising a spirit that is antichrist – meaning *instead of* Jesus Christ. This is one of the signs of the last hour of human history and it is there for all to see. At the end of history there will come a human leader who will set his face against Christ and make a takeover bid for the whole world – a world dictator. Antichrist is coming, but already antichrists are around. What is happening in the world? Why is country after country closing its borders to Christian missionaries? It is because the final battle of history is heading up to the great final struggle between Christ and the devil, between Christ and antichrist. The struggle is building up all the time. Can't you see that happening?

How do the "antichrists" do it? Their most effective way is to get inside churches and disrupt them, by attacking the *doctrine* of Jesus Christ. John is saying that the arrival of these people in our church tells us we are living in the last days of human history, and their departure tells us that they don't really belong. Those who don't believe orthodox Christian things don't stay in an orthodox church very long. They come in, they will try to disrupt, they will try to get people into their views, but sooner or later they will go out and start up their own show. They don't abide. They come in and they go out, and they go out because they are not of us. They don't stay in the fellowship because they have got strange ideas and their funny ideas don't fit in with the truth.

What are these false teachers saying? It may seem to you a bit academic that I should tell you what false doctrine and belief was around in the first century AD, but the book I mentioned earlier, *The Neophiliacs*, finishes up with the same heresy that is here. I find it being produced in and through the mass media. What is this heresy that antichrist preaches? It is that Jesus is not the Christ; that the man Jesus was not God; that the human and the divine were not in him – the physical and the spiritual are too far apart to meet in one person. This is the heresy of sect after sect, and they don't stay within churches, they want you to go and join theirs.

This is the heresy of many a sect that comes knocking at your door today. Ask them if they believe that Jesus is God. Denial of this is the heresy in all Unitarian thinking. John is teaching that this false teaching – that Jesus is not God – is the biggest lie that anyone can ever tell.

Now think that through. What is the biggest lie you ever told? Can you think of it? The biggest lie anyone ever told was that Jesus is not God. Why is it a lie? Because the person who says that is flying in the face of all the evidence. There is no-one with an open mind who will read the story of Jesus and study the evidence who isn't driven to the conclusion: "Truly this man is the Son of God."

John is saying you must not deny the divinity of Jesus. The people who deny that Jesus is the Son of God lose the Father too. If you don't accept the Son you can't find the Father. You are like an orphan in a vast, lonely world; you have got no Father. You may believe in God but he is not Father. You study what the sects call "God". They will call him "Jehovah" and anything but Father.

If you know Jesus as the Son of God, you know God as the Father of Jesus. He that has the Son has the Father. He who denies the Son has not the Father. You can't have one without the other. Either he is the Son of God and God is the Father, or God isn't the Father at all.

The opposite of denying the truth of Christ is confessing it. It is not just to *believe* it but to *confess* it. The heretic uses his mouth to tell you Jesus is not God; then you use your mouth to tell people Jesus *is* God. Whoever confesses the Son has the Father. Tell people that Jesus is the Son of God and you will have the Father with you—that is the promise of eternal life.

Sometimes people come to me and say, "I hear so many interpretations of Christianity, so many different ideas about Jesus, how do I know what is the truth?" John is saying here

that there is a third person involved, there is the teaching
of the Holy Spirit. Here you must be on your guard against
letting your knowledge of truth depend on one human
teacher. You will find that most divisions, most sects, have
started because people have allowed one man to be their sole
judge in matters of faith. If he becomes that, he has usurped
the place of the Holy Spirit. Never quote me against another
teacher. Never say: "David Pawson says, therefore it must be
true." You have no right to say that, and no authority from
me to say it. How do you know if what I say is the truth? Or
if what someone up the road in a hall is saying is the truth?
Do you play one off against the other? Do you ask which
one had the better theological training? You are to ask this
person, the Holy Spirit, who anointed you with the truth, to
tell you in your heart what is the truth. You have a person
inside to help you if you are a Christian. You have, literally,
intuition. You have a tutor inside who gives you tuition in
your heart, and Christians know this to be true. You may be
listening to a man and you say, "There's something wrong
here, this doesn't sound right, this is not true; I don't know
what's wrong with it, and I couldn't argue with him, but it
just doesn't seem right to me." That is the intuition of the
Holy Spirit saying that.

On the other hand, there are times when you say: "I don't
like that man in the pulpit but what he says finds my heart.
There is something there that fits me." It is the Holy Spirit
who is telling you what is true. Every Christian who has had
an anointing of the Holy Spirit knows what is true. "You
have no need for me to teach you," says John.

When you listen to a heresy you may not be able to argue
with the man, but inside the Holy Spirit says, "No, this is
not the truth." Let not anyone be needed to teach you. Of
course, there is need for teachers in the church – that is what
God called me to be, and others. Of course, there is need for

teaching the Word of God. John says, "Abide in what you heard from the beginning." But there is no need for a pope, no need for an infallible preacher to tell you what you must believe and what is certainly true. You can listen to preachers, and if you say at the beginning of the sermon, "O Holy Spirit, tell me what is true in this sermon," you will know by the end. You don't need anyone to teach you the truth, for in the Holy Spirit, who is the spirit of truth, there is no lie at all.

Here then are the two great pressures on us: the pressure to wrong behaviour and the pressure to wrong belief. The pressure to wrong behaviour comes from the world outside the church. The pressure to wrong belief, alas, comes from the world inside the church. You don't listen to the world outside the church when it comes to matters of belief. But the tragedy of our time (and it happened in the first century), is that there are false teachers within the church – wolves in sheep's clothing. How do you recognise them? Remember that the Holy Spirit is the infallible teacher, the one whom every Christian can claim as the teacher to give intuition.

I have been amazed sometimes at the youngest Christian, only a few weeks old, who has been taken to hear false teaching, and they have come back and said, "I don't know what was wrong with it, but there was something wrong." That is the Holy Spirit from the very beginning. Ask the Holy Spirit to make clear to your heart what is true from his Word.

So we confess that Jesus Christ is divine and human, both perfectly together – and to deny that truth is the biggest lie there is. Abide in the truth you had from the beginning. The old gospel is still the only true one. Somebody said to me: "You're a conservative in theology, aren't you?" I said, "Yes I am, and so ought you to be if you're a Christian." We believe in the old gospel. It is still true what you heard from the beginning. If you change it, it is no gospel.

LAWLESS OR RIGHTEOUS?

Read 1 John 2:28 – 3:10

Two thousand years ago the Lord Jesus came to this earth. He was the only person who ever chose to be born, and he came quite deliberately, and he lived here. His visit lasted about thirty-three years. There was a mistake in the calendar and we now know that it was probably from BC 4 to AD 29. Why did he visit this planet? What was his purpose in coming? We shall study this.

When he left after thirty-three years, he left from the Mount of Olives, and as he ascended into the clouds he could look down and see the little town of Bethlehem just seven or eight miles down the road from up there. He stayed within a very small area of the earth. The world can never be the same again.

The other great event of history is his second visit. One of the things the New Testament promises 300 times is that Christ is going to come to this planet again. I find that the most exciting thought: the very same Jesus who came the first time is coming a second. We know how he will come. He will not come the second time as a little baby, he will come as he left, as the full mature man and the Son of God. We know where he will come to because the Bible predicts that he will return to the same spot on earth from which he left – the Mount of Olives – and his feet shall stand on that mountain.

Even more exciting is the promise in the New Testament that when Jesus comes back, every Christian will be gathered from all parts of the world. Even those who are dead will be gathered out of the cemeteries. Those whose ashes are scattered over the face of the earth will be gathered together and they will meet him not on the ground but in the air, which means that every Christian is going to have an aerial trip to the Holy Land. Doesn't that excite you? You will meet him there. We shall look down on the land in which it was all worked out. We shall look on Jerusalem – the old city and the new city. We shall look down on the Sea of Galilee and the Jordan river, but I have the feeling that we won't have eyes for any of that. I have the feeling we will hardly notice it because we shall see Jesus as he is.

Here then are the two great events of world history: the two appearings of Jesus. He has appeared once and he is going to appear a second time. People saw him once two thousand years ago and they will see him again. I know how he is coming, I know where he is coming to, I know why he is coming, but I don't know when. Neither did he, only God the Father knows when Jesus is going to come again. It is the *purpose* of his two visits that occupies us now.

John, writing this letter to his own church as an old man of ninety, the last apostle alive to remember Jesus in the flesh, saw him come the first time and will see him come the second time. Why did he come? Why is he going to come? What difference does it make to our daily life now that Jesus appeared and will appear? We live between the two appearings.

He came the first time to take away sins. He will come the second time to take away saints. You can sum it up in that. Everything else is related to these two purposes. Both times he comes to take away.

In Newcastle, on my grandfather's tombstone, there are three words and an exclamation mark. It is not the usual "Rest in Peace" or such like. He asked that they should put on "What a Meeting!" Many people I have seen look at that gravestone and scratch their heads and think, "Must be a crank buried there." He was a Christian "crank", a "fool for Christ's sake" and a wonderful man. He asked that those words be put there because he lived looking forward to the biggest Christian meeting there will ever be, a meeting of all the Christians dead and alive. Can you reckon how many that would be? No wonder it has to be in the air, there is no other place on earth big enough to hold such a meeting where we could all see Jesus.

This is the meeting to which we look forward, and it will surely be the greatest day for every Christian. Or will it? Some Christians will not feel very happy on that day. One group will be ashamed and the other group will be confident. John uses both words. Let us take the first. Some will be ashamed when they meet him. They will be embarrassed, they won't want to look him in the eye, because while they were on earth they did not abide in Christ. What does abiding in Christ mean? It means staying with him, remaining with him every day of your life. It doesn't just mean being full of enthusiasm when you are young and in your teens and just converted. It means being full of zeal for the Lord when you are forty and fifty and sixty and seventy and eighty. It means getting over that middle-aged hump which is one of the most dangerous spiritual periods of all. It means maintaining the spiritual fire all your life – abiding in Christ.

Others will be confident, and the word means "bold to speak". The word "confidence" in the Bible always means being bold enough to speak to someone. Christians will want to go straight to Jesus and have a word with him. They will want to say, "Lord, here I am, I have always wanted to see what you are like and now I know." They will be eager to come towards him, not shrinking back, they will want to be as close to him as they can, because they did abide in him;

because all their lives on earth they stayed with him; because they never let up; because they never eased up; because they never lost their first love; because they kept their glow for the Lord all their lives.

Don't you know some saints who kept as alert and alive spiritually for forty or fifty years as they were when they first began to love Jesus? Supposing today were the day in which Jesus was coming back, would you be ashamed that you haven't been as close to Christ all your Christian life as you should have been? Or would you be gladly confident as you came into his presence?

John now makes a statement in 2:29 which seems to have no connection at all. So let's look at the statement and find the connection. He suddenly makes two simple statements: *you know that he is righteous*. You know what he is like, he is perfectly good, perfectly honest, perfectly kind, perfectly straight and upright. Therefore, you can know something else: you can be sure that *everyone who does right is born of him*. If you know what Christ is like, you can make sure that everyone who is like Christ is born of Christ – a simple statement. What connection has that with what we have just been thinking about? The answer is that when he appears something is going to happen to us. In one sentence: when we see him as he is, we shall be like him.

Now let me try to draw out the connection and you will see it. We are already different from everybody else in the world. If you are a believer, a Christian, you are already different from others. What is the difference? The answer is that as a believer and a Christian you have a heavenly Father who loves you and calls you his child and tells you that you are his son or daughter . He is your Father and he loves you.

It is not only that he calls us that, we *are* that. See what manner of love the Father has given to us that he calls us his children, and so we are. By our supernatural, heavenly birth, we have become his family. Now here comes the point: by looking at someone, you can't tell that. The world cannot recognise God's children. The world did not recognise that Jesus was the Son of God, so they are certainly not going to recognise that we are sons of God. You cannot tell this difference by looking at a person. Sometimes to the Christian there is an immediate rapport, an understanding, but you could walk right past a Christian in the street and not recognise them as such. But even if you did, the world wouldn't. They can only see a human being. The world will not call you God's children, but God does. What does it matter that the world doesn't know I am a child of God? If God knows it, that is what matters. The world can say, "He's just an ordinary man." But see what love the Father has bestowed on us – he calls us children. The world tries to kid itself that everybody is a child of God, but they are not.

Here is what John is leading up to: we are already different from the world, but when he appears it will be quite obvious who belongs to him. For we shall be like him then and everybody will not only know that Christ is the Son of God, they will know that all the Christians around him are sons of God too. There is coming a day when the difference in appearance between believers and unbelievers will be as obvious as that between sheep and goats. If ever you have seen sheep and goats together, you will know that nobody gets them confused. There is coming a day when believers and unbelievers will look completely different and all will be able to tell the difference.

There are now three wonderful logical statements: first, Jesus will appear visibly, physically in his body. People have all kinds of spiritual, vague ideas about Christ coming. I have heard people say that when you feel he is near, that is his second coming. It is nothing of the kind. When he comes he will appear, we will see him visibly. That is the first thing:

when he appears. You notice it is not *if*, it is "when". It is certain.

Second, we shall see him *as he is*. I want to underline a little word there: "is". You will not see him as he *was*, you will see him as he *is*. You will not see him as the disciples saw him on the roads of Galilee, you will see him as he is now in glory. If you want a description of what he is like now to look at, read Revelation chapter 1. We will see him in his brilliant glory. They caught a glimpse of it once on the mount of transfiguration, but we shall see him as he is.

We shall be exactly like him, and at this point my imagination stops. We are all so different – how could we all be like Jesus? I don't know, but I do know this: when we see him, we shall all be just like him. Physically, we shall have a new body as he got a new body in his resurrection. In character, we shall be just like him – perfect. In glory, we shall shine like him; we shall shine as he once shone on the mount of transfiguration.

I have a lovely little newspaper photograph from my home town Newcastle upon Tyne, taken when King George V visited the town to launch a ship. Afterwards he asked to meet the men who built it. So he went down a long line, shaking hands with a lot of people. Right at the end of the line there was a little "rivet boy", whose job it was to hold a bucketful of rivets and pass them to the riveter. There he was, and he is shown standing there, and the photographer had just caught him shaking hands with the King. The lad is so excited he has got his cap on, having forgotten to take it off, and he is shown beaming – his face is like sunshine. Even though the King's back is to the camera, you can see what he is looking like. You can only see the back of King George's head but you know what his face is like, for it is perfectly reflected in this little boy the day he met the King.

That is what it is going to be like for us. He will appear

visibly, people will see him with eyes. We shall see him as he is, not as he was, and we shall be like him. Then, for the first time, you will be able to pick out every Christian from the whole world. That is going to be a terrible shock for some. On that day when appearances will alter, we will see the connection.

If you really believe that, if you really hope that and expect that will happen to you, what happens? The answer is: he that has this hope in him purifies himself now as he is pure. You want to start getting ready now. If you really want to be like Christ, you want to be like him now. It helps you; it is an incentive, a stimulus to holiness, to believe that you are going to be like that.

The word "purify" means to get rid of pollution. The world is getting terribly worked up about the problem of pollution. But the problem of polluted water is not our main problem. Jesus once said, "It's not what goes into your mouth that makes you dirty, it's what comes out of your mouth that makes you dirty." It is what comes out of your heart that makes you dirty. Envy and covetousness and temper is pollution. There is a terrific pollution problem in the world.

So every Christian who hopes to be like Christ one day gets busy on the pollution problem in his own heart and life, because that is where it starts. I am polluting life now. I am polluting relationships, I am polluting conversation. Since I am going to be like Christ, I want to be like him now. What will happen when we see Jesus? We shall be made completely like him because we are in a mirror reflecting the glory of the Lord and being transformed into the same image. When we have the perfect vision, there will be the perfect reflection, and the image of God will be restored in us. Therefore, as you know that he is righteous, whoever does right is born of him – that is the message. If a person is really looking for Christ's second appearing, they will do something now. They will purify themselves now.

We go back in history to the first appearing of Christ. The word "appeared" comes in again twice in the next section, vv. 4–10. It is referring now to his first appearing – the time that people first saw Jesus, the Son of God. Those who will be changed at his second coming will already have been changed by his first coming. The outward change at the second appearing will be obvious to everybody in the day that our Lord appears. At the moment, you can't tell just by glancing at a person, but you can tell that there has been an inward change because over time there is an outward change in behaviour, and it is by a person's behaviour that you can tell whether the inward change has in fact taken place.

Let us look first at what we must *be* (see vv. 4–7). We must be now one of two sorts of people – either sinners or saints. We are either lawless or righteous now. We have to accept that within the Bible there are no half measures, you are either one or the other. You cannot sit on the fence, you cannot be in the middle – you are either lawless in behaviour or you are righteous. Let us look at what is meant by these two things. It is an individual matter. Look at each life.

First, what is lawlessness? Sin and lawlessness are interchangeable terms. We are sinners, we are lawless ones. Lawlessness means not only that I break the law, it is something much deeper than that. To be lawless is to rebel and say, "I will not have anyone telling me what to do." When we say that a character is lawless we don't mean that he has broken particular laws, we mean that he doesn't recognise any law. He is a law to himself. It is to refuse to recognise any external moral authority over yourself. It is to assert yourself and say: I refuse to submit to my parents, to the laws of society, to the commands of God. Anyone who tells me what to do, I refuse to submit to. Now that is what sin is, and therefore what sin does is to break the law.

Lawlessness becomes lawbreaking. It is because we are lawless that we break the laws. It is because we are sinners that we commit sins. It is because we assert ourselves and won't have other people telling us what to do that we do wrong, and this is what John is saying. This, of course, is the universal state of mankind.

Every one of our children was born with a lawless nature and so were yours. Sooner or later that lawless nature does wrong and breaks someone's command and someone's laws, whether it was the laws of parents, school, society or God. There isn't a man or a woman on earth who hasn't broken someone's laws – because they are lawless; because they don't accept other people's authority over them; because they want to assert their own decisions and their own will.

Now here comes the crunch: why did Jesus appear? He appeared to take away sins—that's all. We can preach Christianity as if all he did was to come to *forgive* sins but that is not true, he came to *take them away*. He didn't just come to get me let off, he came to get me clean. He didn't just come so that he could take away the punishment for my sin, he came to take away the sin. That is why he was given the name "Jesus" because he shall save people from their sins, to take them away. He was the only person who could do so, because in him there was no sin – that is what John is saying.

Jesus had no lawlessness in his person, no rebellion against authority. He submitted to the authority even of the law of Israel and certainly the law of God, and to the law of his parents – he was subject to his father and mother. He submitted all through his life, he was a law-abiding person. In his purpose, he came to help other people be the same, to take away sins.

Now come two logical but startling statements: whoever abides in him does not sin; whoever sins has neither seen him nor known him. Now if you think those are a bit strong, let me repeat them in other words. The presence of Christ in someone's life inevitably means the absence of sin. The presence of sin in someone's life inevitably means the absence of Christ. Why? Because Christ is sinless and he came to take away sins. How can sin and the Saviour live together? They are incompatible; they can't mix.

The presence of sin in a person's life means that Christ is absent and the presence of Christ in someone's life means that sin is absent. Where the Saviour comes, sin goes. It is inevitable. You cannot have both. If you sin tomorrow morning it will be because at that point you do not have the Saviour with you and you are not abiding in him. You cannot possibly have both, they just don't go together.

Therefore, and we can now state it positively, he who does right is righteous as he is righteous—there comes the statement again. We are saved to live a righteous life, which means a right life – to live right, to do right, to be right as he was right, and there can be no compromise whatsoever. In other words, you can tell that someone is *abiding* in Christ – they do right. You can tell someone who *knows* Christ – they do right. You can tell someone who has *seen* Christ – they do right. You can tell someone who doesn't know Christ: they assert themselves; they do what they want; they rebel against anyone telling them what to do; they are self-determined people. You can tell straight away by studying behaviour.

But now we come on to something further, vv. 8–10: what we cannot be. Behind the behaviour lies a nature and behind the nature lies a parent. Our behaviour comes from our nature, our nature comes from our parent. My children were born lawless in nature because their dad and their mum were lawless by nature. Their behaviour becomes lawless and there is a problem to us from time to time because of the nature that we gave them—that is a vicious circle.

Somebody wrote to me: "You know, the trouble with having children is you see your own faults appearing in them." I understood what they meant. It is one of the tragedies of parenthood in a fallen world that we produce fallen children. The parent gives the nature and the nature leads to the behaviour. This is why sometimes parents give way to the temptation not to discipline their children because they can see that ultimately they gave them that nature.

There are only two families in the whole human race: the children of the devil and the children of God. There is no other family in the whole world, and each father has passed on to his children his nature, and that nature will lead to a certain behaviour. It is inevitable – the one leads to the other. The devil will give you a nature like his own and he sinned from the beginning and you will, and God gives you his nature, and whoever is born of God cannot sin.

I will tell you what that means in a moment, but first of all let us consider the devil. There is a devil, a supernatural, evil being who has millions of children in this world. You can meet them on every bus, every tube train. You can't tell just by looking, but there are children of God and children of the devil. One day we will see the difference just by looking, but now you can't. How do you tell the difference? You study behaviour, and this is what you find: children of the devil behave just like the devil; they are "chips off the old block". He rebelled from the beginning. From the very beginning he said: God, I'm having my own show, I'm not going to have you run my life. Anybody who is a child of the devil says just the same. They say it to their parents, they say it to their schoolteachers, they will say it to the police, they will say it to anyone, "I'm not having you tell me what to do." They'll say it to the traffic wardens; they will park on the double yellow lines and be defiant. It is as simple as this: that a child of the devil does what the devil does and says,

"God, society, parents, you're not going to run my life." He did this from the very beginning and you notice that it says the devil is still doing it. Every day the devil rebels against God; every day the devil sins.

But now let us come to the other side of it. Why did Jesus appear? He appeared to put the devil out of business. Isn't that lovely? He appeared to destroy the works of the devil. Hebrews 2:15 tells you that because we were in bondage to Satan and death, Jesus took flesh and blood that he might deliver those who all their lifetime were subject to bondage.

What is the devil's business? With your body to fill you with disease, with your mind to fill you with error, and with your soul to fill you with sin. That is his business, and his business has succeeded tremendously. He is in big business, he has got most of the world in that business – until Jesus came to smash the devil's business and put him out of work. Jesus started doing it in the days of his flesh and has been doing it ever since. He visited our earth to smash Satan's hold on human nature. We were born into the devil's family and are sons of the devil. Jesus came that we might have new life, becoming God's children. Now here is a very strong statement: *no-one born of God commits sin*. Some have seen perfectionism in this verse. Quite frankly, though, it is not there, because that would mean that as soon as you become a Christian you must be perfect, and that if you are not then you are not a Christian. It cannot mean that because in this very letter John has said to Christians that if you say you don't sin you are a liar. He also said that if anyone sins we have an advocate. But here is the thing and unfortunately it doesn't come out too clearly in the English but it is there in the Greek, and it comes out in many modern translations now that we understand these verbs: the verbs in chapters 2 and 3 are in a different tense. In chapter 2, where it says "If anyone sins" the verb means an occasional, isolated, individual act, whereas the verbs in chapter 3 are all in the continuous present tense, which means to go on doing something. Therefore, this letter does say that Christians may fall occasionally into sin, but it also says that they cannot live in it habitually. If I can re-translate or paraphrase 3:9, "No-one born of God can go on committing sin." In other words, the habitual life of someone born of God is to do good, to do right, to make progress in the Christian life. The habitual life of the child of the devil is to do wrong. The child of the devil occasionally does right, the child of God occasionally does wrong, and the Bible explains why.

The Christian can fall into sin but he cannot walk in it. The Christian can lapse into sin but he cannot live in it—he cannot go on like that. Therefore the proof that a man is born of God is that he does not go on living as he did. He may occasionally fall, but I'll tell you what will happen: he will be stricken with remorse and come back in repentance, and be picked up by God and go on. This verse is not teaching perfection, it is teaching progress. It is saying that the change will become more and more obvious.

The Greek here says, literally, that when a man is born of God the *sperma* stays in him – Greek for the seed or sperm of God. Can I put it like this: a person born of God has become pregnant with Christ; God's sperm is in him; God's life is in him, and just as with a pregnant woman there is an inevitable progress – and people will begin to notice that something is happening, that she is different.

So Paul says, "Christ is being formed within you." Sooner or later it will show and the person will become different in behaviour. They will do right whereas once they did wrong. They will come towards God whereas once they ran away from God. They will get less self-assertive instead of more self-assertive – it is bound to happen. Therefore I emphasise this: no-one born of God can go on committing sin, for God's seed abides in him and he cannot go on sinning because he's born of God.

It is all tied up with the first and second comings of Christ. He came to take away sins, therefore if we don't follow him in righteousness we don't know him, we don't abide in him, we have never seen him. He will come again and complete what he has begun and we shall be like him. Then everyone will see us as we really are because we shall have seen him as he really is.

A CHILD OF GOD

Read 1 John 3:11–24

John is writing this little letter for one reason: that everybody may be quite sure what is a Christian and whether they are one. The most important question you can ever ask is, "Am I a Christian?" The second most important question is when you meet others: "Is he or she a Christian?" How do you tell if you are? How do you tell if they are? There are deceptions going on in the world. There is an awful lot of profession about that is not real. There are a lot of false Christians around who say they are Christians but are not. How do you tell?

John now moves on to two simple tests. I put them in simple English first, and then you have got them. If you really are a child of God then two things will happen: you will take after your Father and you will take to your brethren – it is bound to happen. If these two things do not appear in your life, then you are not a child of God even if you say you are and have been baptised and go to church. You may go to communion, you may read your Bible, you may give money to the poor, but unless you take after your Father and take to your brethren you are not a child of God.

We are going to look at these two things. Let me now give them two rather longer titles that fit in with the passage. Taking the second point first: the first sign of a true Christian is compassion towards his earthly brother or sister. The second sign of a true Christian is confidence before his heavenly Father. I would ask you very directly these two questions. Have you got compassion toward your earthly brothers? Have you got confidence before your heavenly Father? If so, you are a son of God, and a brother or sister of mine. If not, you are not a child of God and you will not go to live with God in his heavenly home.

From the very beginning of Christianity there has been an emphasis on love. This is the one word that Christianity brought to life in the ancient world, a world where there was precious little love, where there was lust of all kinds. Out of the fifteen Roman emperors, fourteen were homosexual. Of the marriages that took place in the Roman empire in the days of our Lord, three-quarters ended in divorce. There was precious little real love in the world into which Jesus came.

But among Christians there was such an emphasis on love that people exclaimed, "Look how these Christians love each other." The early Christians were like a cluster of chaste snowdrops growing on a foul rubbish heap [I am quoting from a contemporary writer] because they loved one another. Let us get this right, the new thing that they brought into being was not only love for God—that had been there in the Old Testament days; not just love for neighbour—that had been there in the old Testament. On the last night before he died Jesus gave his disciples a new commandment. They already knew that you should love God with all your heart and soul and mind and strength, and your neighbour as yourself. Here is the new one: "By this will all men know that you are my disciples, that you love one another. A new commandment I give you, that you love one another." In other words, the first acid test of whether a man or a woman is a real Christian is their attitude to other Christians.

Now of course, there are other Christians we may find it difficult to like. I am thankful that the Bible uses the word "love", not the word "like". You can learn to love someone before you like them, and loving them will lead you to like them. You try praying for someone you dislike every day and see how long it takes for you to like them. But in praying for them, you love them.

Do you love your earthly brother? If I really know God, then every earthly brother of mine I meet, every fellow Christian – I love. I may not be able to speak his language, I may never have seen him before but he is my long lost brother; he is the one I have never seen but is part of the family.

To make this quite clear, John now draws a contrast between brotherly hate and brotherly love. At this point he goes back to a terrible story to show you the opposite of brotherly love. He goes back to the story of the first death in human history, and it was not an accidental death or a death of old age but murder. What a dreadful indictment of the human race. How did it take place? There were two brothers in the same family and one hated the other. It started in his heart. Deliberate murder begins inside before ever the hand is raised.

Inside Cain's heart there grew up a horrible thing called envy. I don't know if you understand what envy is. It is one of the most awful cancers of the human heart there is, eating away true affection. What is envy? It is resentment that somebody else is better off than you are, that's all. Envy operates like this: you never envy somebody who is far away from you. It's always someone who is near. Let me give you an illustration: a Sunday school teacher doesn't envy the great Sunday school expert who comes down to give lectures and who is obviously a great one at it. The Sunday school teacher will envy the other Sunday school teacher in her department who seems to have a bigger class and have much more fun with the children and gets the lesson across. A Christian singer will not envy one of the great international singers though they may admire them and want to emulate them. They envy the other singer in the church who was chosen to sing at the special service instead of them. You see how envy works? It works on someone who is a potential rival, someone who is in the same business and could take your place. Cain and Abel came to God together side by side. Cain brought a gift to God but he didn't bring himself. He didn't bring his love; he just brought a gift, a subscription. But Abel brought a gift that expressed his love, and God said, "Abel, I'll take your gift, but Cain I can't have yours." Cain was envious and angry because his brother was better off.

Hatred always thinks of those who are better off; love always thinks of those who are poorer – that is the difference. Who are the people you think of most, those who have got more than you have or those who have less than you have? That tells you whether you love or hate. So Cain envied Abel and he not only envied him because he was better off but – notice this – he envied him because he was better. From the beginning of history, bad people hate good people. Those who are better as well as better off are those who are hated by those who are sons of the devil.

Now because this malice was in his heart, the next thing was that he raised his hand and murdered, which is why Jesus taught that you may never have stuck a knife into someone's back, you may never have killed them with a blow, but if you hated them you are a murderer. That is one of the most terrifying things Jesus ever said. If you are angry with someone or call them a fool, you wish them dead so you are a murderer. You are a son of the devil; you are like Cain. Cain hated his brother; he murdered him. You may not have murdered a person, but if you hate him you are a murderer.

Then we have the statement: "Brethren, Christians, don't be surprised if the world hates you." It hated Christ, why? Because he was better. It will hate Christians. Why? Because they are better. Occasionally someone comes to me and says, "I don't understand it: I am really trying to love my family. I don't preach at them. I'm a Christian, I'm the only Christian in the family but I don't try to throw my religion at them. I really want to be a better wife or husband to my partner, a better parent to my children. I really try to go out of my way and they seem to dislike me for it; they hate me for it."

Or somebody comes to me and says: "In my office I'm the only Christian. I try to help other people. I try to be kind to them, but they don't like me and they don't mix with me. They don't go out with me." They are surprised. Don't be surprised; don't wonder at this. Why? A son of the devil will always hate a son of God who is better than he is. It is a challenge. This is why they will try to take it out of you.

In the RAF I used to notice Christian boys who came into a billet. Twenty men in a billet were all living at very close quarters, and one boy came in who lived at a much higher level than they did. He didn't swear, he didn't waste his money on things that were just no use to him or anyone else. He lived clean and he didn't join in the dirty jokes. What happened? They hated him. They tried to knock it out of him. They mocked him; they laughed at him. Remember how people spat on and crucified Jesus.

The great Greek philosopher Socrates, who lived many years before Jesus was born, said, "If ever a perfect man lives in this world, he will be murdered." Socrates was a wise man, and he could see that sons of the devil hate sons of God; bad people dislike good people. That is hatred, and when you hate someone you want to take life from them. You look at them and see they have more than you have and you want to rob them of it.

Let us turn to the opposite and look at love – it is as different as death and life. We know that we have passed from death to life because we don't hate people any more. We love the brethren, and what does love do? Instead of taking life from people, it gives life to people. Instead of striking down life, it lays down life. Instead of murdering, it ministers. That is the difference, and of course our example is Christ.

I am sorry that the phrase "laid down their life" is so abused. It is put on every war memorial. Now I hope I don't offend anyone, but I'm going to quote now from the controversial film called *Patton*, about General Patton of the American army. In one of the scenes before going into battle, General Patton says this, "Now lads, let's have no silly talk about laying down our lives for our country. Your job is to make the other chap lay down his life for his country." That is about the most honest thing I've ever heard said about war. Within a war there are a few who lay down their lives, but most men who go to war, though they know the risk, hope that they will get back and they are determined to make the other chap lay down his life for his country. So let's be careful how we use the phrase, "lay down life." I'll tell you of a man I know who did. Come with me to a Japanese prisoner of war camp in Malaya. There one day the Japanese commandant said that something had been done which was a serious crime against the Japanese empire. He said, "Until the person owns up who has done it – and he will be shot – then the officers will be kept as hostages and will be shot the following day." So the officers were put in solitary confinement and kept, and the men put in the blazing sun on the parade ground of the prisoner of war camp, and no-one spoke. The commandant said again, "Unless the person who did that owns up, these officers die tomorrow." But nobody spoke until the chaplain said, "I did it." He stepped forward, and the officers were released, and the chaplain was shot there and then, but he had not done it. Now that is laying down one's life.

I will tell you what laying down one's life is. It is when you are absolutely free to keep it. It is not when somebody takes it from you – that is not laying down your life, it is when you quite voluntarily, knowing what you do, for the sake of someone else, put yourself in their place. Real love, as opposed to hatred, lays down its life for the brethren. That was what Jesus did. He was only thirty-three. We often forget that he was a very young man with all his life stretching ahead of him, with all the popularity, with all the greatness there, and yet he laid down his life. He could have kept it, but he set his face to go to Jerusalem and he laid it down.

We may not be called upon to make a heroic sacrifice, but there is another way of laying down your life. There is the heroic way and there is the humdrum way. How do you lay down your life in a humdrum way? I will tell you: if anyone sees his brother in need and has this world's goods to give him and closes his heart, then he is not laying down his life. If you see someone in need and say, "I can help you in that need, here's some money, here are some clothes," then you are laying down your life.

In other words, hatred robs somebody else of their most precious possession, life, but love gives to somebody else your precious possessions, the world's goods. That is called "laying down your life" in scripture. It is twice said in the Gospel of John that Jesus laid down his life, or laid down something. The first is when he washed people's dirty, smelly feet. Jesus did that the night before he died. It says, "He laid down his garments, and he washed their feet."

Then the next day they stripped his clothes off him and he laid down his life. In other words, you can lay down your life for the brethren in a multitude of ways. If there is somebody you meet tomorrow in need and you are able to help them and have more than they have got and you give them something to help them, then you have laid down your life for the brethren. You can do it every day, sometimes it is harder to do it in life than to do it in death, but we are called to do both. This, then, is love. Hatred of a brother robs him, resents the fact that he has got more. Love for the brother says, "I've got more, let me help you. Let me give, let me rob myself." Which are we doing? Which is the attitude in your life? This is the first fundamental test. Actions speak louder than words.

The other mark of the true Christian is that he has confidence before God. This irks and irritates the sons of the devil. Nothing irritates the unbeliever more than the confidence of the believer. He will say, "Oh, you're so sure of yourself, aren't you? It's conceit." But this confidence is not self-confidence. John goes on to acknowledge that there are times in the Christian life when your heart condemns you, when you are most unsure of yourself. Is that not true? I know that the front you present to the world, and what the world sees of you, is a certain, confident, sure Christian, but is it not true that in your heart of hearts there are times when your heart says, "Are you?" Are there moments when your heart condemns you, saying: "You wouldn't do that if you were a Christian." There may be moments when you come before God and say, "Oh God, I'll never be a saint." A Christian can be terribly unsure of himself yet confident before God. He will have inward questions, perhaps moments when he doesn't feel that he is right with God, but he doesn't put his confidence in his feelings. He is aware that God knows better and knows everything. He knows that God knew the worst about him when he accepted him. Isn't that wonderful? You make earthly friends, and when they get to know more about you they drift away. You make an earthly friend, and they discover something about you they never knew existed and that cools it off. But even though I am unsure of myself, I have got confidence before God because he knew the worst, he knows everything.

There is a lovely example of this in the Bible. One night Peter swore that he didn't know Jesus. He said, "I don't know him. I swear I don't," and it was his best friend he was talking about. Peter's heart condemned him and he went out and wept. A few days later he met Jesus on the seashore at Galilee. He looked at Jesus, and Peter's heart condemned him. He didn't know what to say about his denial, but he said, "Jesus, you know everything. You know that I love you." That is the important thing.

Jesus knows that I love him even though I may have done this thing. He knows that I may have denied him, but I hate myself for doing it and I weep. He knows everything; he knows that I love him. So we have confidence before God and it is not because we feel that we are great or that we are better than anyone else.

An unbeliever doesn't have a heart that condemns them. I have noticed that it is the Christians whose hearts condemn them. It is the Christian who says "I am the chief of sinners." It is the Christian who says "I'm too bad for God to take notice of" – yet he is still confident because he knows that God knew this, and that God loves him and that God has called him his child, so he has confidence.

This shows in an obedient life but it shows first in prayer. The confidence of a child of God in prayer is completely different from the prayer of a son of the devil. Sons of the devil do pray – most people pray either with formal habit or if they are in a real emergency, but do they have confidence? "Whatever we ask we receive from him" – that is confidence in prayer. My children when they were little would run up to me sometimes and ask for something with confidence. They came believing that they would get it, and that is why they came to me. "Daddy, will you come and do this? Daddy, will you mend that?" They don't come wondering, "Well, it's worth trying as a last resort. He might do it." I am afraid sometimes that did happen when I was very busy. But normally when they came you could tell by the tone of their voices. They were confident they were coming to their father and they expected they would get something. So they said, "Daddy, will you mend this? Daddy, will you put this bicycle pump right?" So they came.

Now if you are a child of God, you have confidence in prayer. You don't come as a last resort. You don't say, "Well, we've tried everything else; we might as well try prayer now. It might do something." That is the worldly prayer, the unbelievers' prayer, but if you listen to a real saint of God praying, there is a confidence there. I think of a dear old lady who lived in a caravan in Yorkshire. I used to visit her and we always had a lovely prayer together. She always prayed for me. I asked her to do so. She would pray for certain things, then before she got off her knees, she would say, "And Lord, thank you for those things." That is why she always got an answer. I have never known anyone who could pray like it. She just came like a little child and said, "Daddy, we need this. Thank you for giving it to us," and it came within a few days. This was a wonderful experience.

If you are a son of God you will have confidence in our Father, but there is a condition: that we are keeping his commandments and pleasing him. There is no shortcut to answered prayer. Some people think prayer is just like a slot machine: pop it in and pull the answer out. Prayer never was like that. But if you are a child of God and walking in ways that please him, then you will get it.

Isn't that true to family life? If your children are in a particularly bad mood and misbehaving and just not doing what you want them to and what we have asked them to do, and then they come and say, "Daddy, will you please do this?" My attitude is very different. Of course it is, because our relationship is a moral one. The heavenly Father, if we are not pleasing him, doesn't say, "Oh fine, I'd love to answer your prayer." But when we are walking before him in righteousness and goodness as he wants us to live as his children, then we receive whatever we ask. That is an astonishing claim. I have never yet met an unbeliever who would say "I receive whatever I ask in prayer." I have not met many believers who would say it, but John does. He is teaching that if you are a child of God you can have this confidence if you are pleasing him and in the centre of his will. What is his will? We are told in 3:22–23 and it cuts down to pint-size the understanding that so many people have, that all God wants from us is to be kind to grandmother and the cat. It is amazing how many people think this way, that if you do a good deed a day like the good boy scout, if you help the neighbour when they are in trouble, that is all that God wants from you. I will tell you what pleases God: that you believe in Christ and love Christians. That is what it says here. When someone says "I can be as good a Christian outside the church as those inside" that is a lie. How can he be? How can he "love one another" and remain outside the church? I would question whether he loves Christ much either.

If you are really going to please God, and be a real Christian, and be where he wants you to be so that your prayers can be answered, it involves believing in Jesus and loving his people. If that is where you are, then prayer becomes real. The best meeting is where Christians love each other and pray, and the prayer is confident because of that. If you don't say your prayers out of faith and love then they are empty and hollow and probably pretty selfish too. But when you are pleasing God, by believing in Jesus and loving Christians, then prayer is a bold, confident thing.

So, finally, we come to the end of this passage. If we are keeping his commandments, believing Christ, loving Christians, there is a relationship between us and God that is as close as this: we live in him; he lives in us. God is our home and we are his home – you live together. I remember during the days of my courtship it was lovely to meet my wife. I would travel miles; I would stay up till all hours. I would walk home in the early hours in the morning and think nothing of it. I am not sure I would do that today, but I did then! Oh, it was lovely and I used to go all these miles, rain or all sorts of weather – unlike the young man who said to his girl, "I'd go through earth, air, fire, and water for you, and I'll meet you next Thursday provided it's not raining."

I looked forward to the day when we could live together and make our home with each other. In the same way, a spasmodic meeting with God is just tantalising; a service in which you feel he is real, a meeting in which he comes to you, is tantalising, it just whets your appetite. What do you really want? You want to abide in him and have him abide in you so that Monday morning is as great as Sunday night and the kitchen sink becomes an altar. You can have that by keeping in his will, obeying his commandments, having confidence toward him.

In the last verse we come to the final thing that tells us that we can know that he abides in us. How do we know that God is with us? Because his Spirit is given to us. God is actually living in our hearts through the Holy Spirit and that is why we can love the brethren. Here are the two things that tell me that I belong to God: that I love the brethren (what I am able to give to others); and that I have the Holy Spirit (he is able to give to me).

Which came first? He gave me the Spirit before I loved anyone else. That is how it happened: the love of God is shed abroad in our hearts through the Holy Spirit given to us. This then is what a real Christian is – someone who has been given the Holy Spirit to live within their heart and therefore two things happen: he takes after his Father and he takes to his brother. He has compassion toward his earthly brother and he has confidence before his heavenly Father. If you are not a true Christian it would be better at the last if you had never been born.

"GOD IS LOVE"

Read 1 John 4:1–21

The biggest battle in the world today is not a military one, but a mental one. It is the battle for the mind, because people know perfectly well that as a man thinks in his heart so is he. Your thoughts are going to make your character. Your thoughts are going to determine your behaviour. If you can capture someone's mind, you have got them. Therefore there is a battle going on for people's minds. The big struggle is between ideals, ideas or ideologies. Ideological forces are battling for your mind and your thoughts, and for the minds and thoughts of everybody living in the world. Our minds are being bombarded with new ideas through words in the ear and pictures in the eye. So we may be bewildered by the number of different notions and ideologies being presented to us.

There are two levels at which this battle is going on: the human level and the supernatural level. At the human level the battle is one we call the battle of propaganda. At the supernatural level, the battle is what we call the battle of prophecy. Our study now is concerned with the battle of prophecy for the minds of people. Propaganda comes from human sources, human ideas – one mind trying to influence others – but prophecy comes from supernatural sources and tries to capture the mind.

Before moving to the subject of prophecy, we will think about propaganda. Human beings are constantly trying to control each other's thoughts for various purposes, including the commercial and military. The two great channels of ideas into your mind are the eye and the ear. Formerly the ear was the main channel, and through the spoken word ideas were conveyed to the mind. The great switch in the twentieth century was from the ear to the eye. First the cinema then television did it. The invention of printing, which was able to disseminate propaganda quickly, had led to new ideas being presented to millions of human minds. But television presented a channel for disseminating ideas which was unparalleled in history because, generally speaking, one in the eye is worth two in the ear. Then, of course, the development of the personal computer, the internet and the world wide web developed, and nowadays through the electronic devices in your home and your pocket you are being presented with idea after idea. There are as many ideas as there are people. Every discussion, every blog, every online chat is bombarding you with someone else's notion, and there is a battle of propaganda.

One of the ways in which Satan keeps people from the truth is by suggesting to them that there are so many different aspects and ideas that you will never come to the truth. This constant bombardment, even of religious ideas, is leading people to say, "Well, how do I know who's right? I am just confused. I listen to a preacher on Sunday. I turn my television on and watch a religious programme there and they say something else. I read a book or a magazine and they say something else again. I'm bewildered." But when Christians find Jesus Christ they cease to be sceptical about the possibility of finding out what truth is. No longer do they say what Pilate said cynically, "What is truth?" as much as to say "Who knows?" When you find Jesus and discover he is the truth, you have within yourself an inbuilt resistance to propaganda.

One of the reasons why Christians in communist countries have been hated by the authorities is this resistance to propaganda – they know what is the truth. Read Richard Wurmbrand's books. How was he able to get through brainwashing, torture, degradation and loneliness and still have a firm grasp of Christ? It was because in Christ he found the truth. When you have the truth, propaganda cannot break through. Jesus is the answer to the bewildering variety of propaganda.

Why is this? The answer is that truth does not come by human discovery, it comes by divine revelation. Real truth is not something that people think up. It is something that existed even before people were here on earth, and it is spoken to us by the one who is truth. So many people have discovered that a discussion group which simply pulls in human ideas gets nowhere. Maybe you have joined such a group, and for the first few times it was very interesting, and then you found out what everybody's ideas were and after that it went dead. Why? Because you were simply discussing human ideas and that is a dead end, it is not the way to truth. Whoever said that a discussion group is simply a method of pooling your ignorance was not far off the truth. But when a group of people come together to listen to what God says and to discuss his truth, then the thing goes on being alive; then the group has something to feed on because it is getting truth the right way – by prophecy rather than propaganda. There is nothing worse than a group that is simply each person airing his own views for the others. Who is interested in just listening to other people's ideas? It is boring, but when God says, "This is truth," that is fascinating.

Therefore the gospel is not so much a subject for propaganda but for propagation, for proclamation, for preaching. It is not a discussable thing; it is not a thing that is set as an opinion against other opinions. It is not another idea thrown into the pool of human ideas. It is the truth that is thrown into a whirlpool of propaganda, and this truth stands by itself. That is why, as Paul says to the Corinthians, we do not stoop to subtle methods of propaganda in proclaiming the gospel. We don't try to brainwash, we don't try to manipulate people's minds. We don't try to bombard them with truths so that they cannot refuse it. What do we do? We preach Christ and him crucified, and that is the truth. We don't need to bombard people with propaganda.

We don't need subliminal advertising. Do you know what that is? I was in a coffee shop once and talked to the manager. I said, "I notice you have music playing all the time. Is that to help people sort of relax and eat more?"

"No," he replied, "I'll tell you what it is. There are messages being subliminally flashed in among the music telling you what to buy today. If we have more of this than that in the kitchen, we just put a message on the music and you do not know that the music is telling you what to buy." If you went into that place you were going to be bombarded with propaganda telling you to buy this or that. We do not stoop to that, we don't need to. My job is not to propagandise but to preach the truth. You are free to reject it or accept it, but no-one is going to force you.

Now we turn to something else. If truth comes by prophecy from God rather than propaganda from men, and Christians have in them the one who is the truth, and therefore have a built-in resistance to propaganda, how is the devil going to destroy Christians? How is he going to attack the church? Not by propaganda because Christians don't respond to that, but by false prophecy, through someone bringing claims to be inspired supernaturally saying he is in touch with the other world – someone who will bring messages from that other world, claiming to be from God.

Therefore John is most anxious about his Christian children here. He says: I don't want you to believe every supernatural message; you must not believe every spirit.

This is the one thing that can confuse Christians. Propaganda doesn't, prophecy does. This is one of the growing dangers to Christians in this country – false prophets.

Let us look a little further at this. Christians are not gullible fools. Most people think that Christians would believe anything, that like Alice in Wonderland they believe six impossible things before breakfast every day. That is not true, we are not gullible. We are not guilty of credulity. We are suspicious, we are cautious. We do not believe everything people tell us, even if the person says it came straight from God. We do not believe it, we test it. Christians have a resistance to false prophecy as well as to propaganda. In this we follow Christ. There is a lot of misunderstanding about Christ. Let me say two things about him that you may never have heard preached. Christ did not put his faith in people. It is not a Christian thing to do to believe in other men and women. Knowing your own heart, knowing what the Bible says about human nature, we do not put our faith in people. It says in John's Gospel that Jesus would not trust himself to any man, for he knew what was in men. Jesus was very cautious about this. It is one of the meanings of his phrase "Don't cast your pearls before swine" – don't trust them with holy things.

Secondly, Jesus would not commit himself or trust the spirits, even when they acknowledged him. Time and again the evil spirits said, "We know who you are, you are the Holy One of Israel, you are the Holy One of God," and he said, "Get into those pigs and get out." He wouldn't trust either men or spirits because he was and is the truth. Christians must rightly be cautious and even suspicious before they trust a person or a spirit who tells them something is God's word.

I emphasise that you must be as cautious of me as you would be of anyone else. If I say such and such a thing is true and of the Spirit, you must test that. You must not put your faith in me, and you must test it by the right way and the right test. If it is true then you can say that I said something that was true, but you must not say it until you have tested it for yourself. This is a Bible warning against Christians accepting anybody as infallible. This is the fundamental reason why Christians oppose accepting either a human being or a spirit as infallible. Only God is infallible, test everybody else. Whether it is David Pawson or the Pope or anybody – test it. You have the right and duty to do so.

Why is it that in our Lord's day, there was an outburst of evil spirits? The answer is because the Holy Spirit was doing something new. Now, in this country, the Holy Spirit is doing more and evil spirits are doing more; the battle is being joined more fiercely, as it is in other parts of the world. Therefore I beg you, before you run after someone who claims to be speaking the word of God, test and follow only the truth.

How do you test? Before we go into vv. 1–6, let me summarise the five basic assumptions behind this passage. First, there is such a thing as supernatural prophecy as well as natural propaganda – there are vertical messages from the supernatural, as well as horizontal messages from human minds. Second, therefore there are spirits as well as human beings. There are other beings in the world apart from human ones, intelligent beings who can talk. Third, there are bad spirits and it is vital to know when that is what you are dealing with. Because you have got through to a spirit, that does not mean you are through to God. The supernatural is not necessarily divine, it can be demonic. Fourth, there are therefore false prophets as well as true prophets. A man or a woman can speak immediately inspired by God, and a man or a woman can speak inspired by Satan; the same person could do both. Remember Simon Peter. Jesus said to him, "Who do you say I am?" And Simon Peter said, "You are the Christ, the Son of the living God." Jesus said, "God told you to say that." It was not something Peter thought up. A few minutes later Simon Peter said, "You shall never die." Jesus had to say to Peter, "Get behind me, Satan." It was not the Father speaking in Peter's mouth then, it was Satan. Test! The fifth thing is this: false prophets will be inside the church as well as in the world.

If you don't agree with any of those five things, then you are going to have problems with the rest of what I want to affirm here. But Jesus, Paul, Peter and John made this clear. They used the same words. There will come in among you wolves in sheep's clothing. In other words, you won't be able to tell them by their appearance. They will look just like Christians. How do you tell them?

1 John 4:1–3 describes false prophecy. They tell you to listen to what comes out of their mouths. Don't look at them, they have sheep's clothing. What comes out of their mouths? John begins, "Beloved...." That seems such a contradiction to some people. Some would say that the kind of teaching I am giving here is unloving. They would say, "Surely if you love people you should be tolerant." Never! Love and tolerance are never put together in the scripture; they are enemies. Love and truth go together, and if you love someone you hate error, you hate it like poison because it can capture minds and ruin them.

Therefore, if you really love someone you will tell them what not to believe as well as what to believe. Again I mention that sometimes people say to me, "I wish you'd stick to positive things and tell us what is right rather than condemning what is wrong. Or tell us what to believe instead of telling us what not to believe; defend the faith but don't attack other things." But John is telling readers what they shouldn't believe because he loves them.

If you really love someone then you protect them from poison. If I tell my children, "Don't drink that water, it's full of germs," it is because I love them. If I tell a church, "Don't believe this kind of thing, it's wrong, it's false, it is evil and it is of the devil," it is because I love them. Love and truth are partners, not love and tolerance. Love doesn't tolerate anything. If you don't stand for something, you will fall for anything. It is love that wants to make clear that you understand the difference.

So love says "Don't believe...." If you love someone you will tell them, "Do believe this, don't believe that." Beloved, don't believe every spirit. It doesn't say, "Don't believe any spirit." Believe not every spirit, because there are a lot of false prophets that have gone out into the world. Superstition will believe anything, suspicion will believe nothing; the Christian tests. We are not superstitious, we don't believe *anything*. But we do believe in the Lord and we believe in prophecy, and we believe that God can speak today as he spoke in ancient times. When people say to me, "What do you think about so and so, there's something in it isn't there?" my answer is, "Yes, there's something in it, that's why I don't believe it." Because there is something in it that does not mean you should believe it. People say, "Well, I went along and there is something in it. There's more than just the human in it." I say, "Yes, there's something dangerous in it. Don't touch it. Get away from it if you possibly can." It is because there is something in it, something wrong, that it is dangerous.

After this very timely word of caution, what is the test that will prevent us from accepting any human being as infallible? You can't tell by their appearance—they are in sheep's clothing. You can't even tell by whether they have a Bible in their hands or not, because spirits can quote scripture. Even the devil knows the Bible well enough to misquote it. So if someone has a Bible in his hand, that doesn't tell you if he is a false prophet. If he uses the word

"God" or even the word "Jesus" that doesn't tell you. What is the test?

A Christian friend of mine was in business with a retired army major (not a believer) who asked my friend, "What do you think about spiritism?"

"I take it very seriously," he replied, "because there are such things as spirits, and there are good ones and evil ones and it is very important to tell the difference."

The major asked, "Well, how do you tell the difference?"

My friend just opened the New Testament he carried in his pocket and showed him this verse, "Every spirit which confesses that Jesus Christ has come in the flesh is of God," and said, "You just ask them that."

The major never let on, but his wife had been going to a meeting for some time and had persuaded him to go along that night for the first time, and he did go although he was feeling a little apprehensive. They got some impressive messages which must have come from supernatural sources for they betrayed a knowledge that nobody down here could possibly have had. Then the major was asked, "Would you like to ask anything? Would you like to have a message?" And he said yes. He wasn't a Christian, but he remembered the words, "Ask if Jesus Christ has come in the flesh," and this was passed on. The lady medium went into a terrible state, she went berserk, and the major said, "In all my years in the army I never heard such foul blasphemies as came out of that woman's lips. People were getting up and running for the door." And he said, "My wife will never go there again."

Now that is a simple test. Has Jesus Christ come in the flesh? What does that statement mean? It means the human and the divine were perfectly united in Christ. He is God; he is man. Jesus of Nazareth is the Christ of glory. The eternal Son of God is now the Son of Man. Jesus Christ has combined in himself the two. You find that spirits will not admit this. They either say he is less than fully human or they say he is less than fully divine. They will not say he is both perfectly—he is God, he is man, both – and you can test.

What about this phrase "has come in the flesh"? That means two things. First, that he existed long before Jesus was a man. He was born; he *came*. He always said, "I came". He existed from all eternity. He was there all along and he just came in the flesh, but the other thing it means, which you may not have realised, when it says "has come in the flesh" is that he is still in the flesh; he has never left it. I meet even church members who have not fully realised this and who have got the idea that when Jesus ascended he stopped being human and went back to being divine, but that is not true. Jesus is a human being today with a human body. He has come in the flesh. There is only "one Mediator between God and men, the man Christ Jesus." We have a high priest who is touched with our infirmities because he is human, and that is why I don't need any other priest.

Now here is the test: "Is Jesus of Nazareth the Christ of glory, and is he still in the flesh? Did he rise in the body? Did he eat fish? Did they touch him? When he comes back again will he still have that body? Will we see the nail prints?"

Is Jesus, the one we talk about, both God and man in one person? It is a mystery and my mind cannot grasp it logically. How can he be both? But that is the truth. Only God the Holy Spirit can tell you that, and only God the Holy Spirit can convince you of it. Other spirits deny it and they will not confess it. You know that the Antichrist is to come into the world. The devil's last masterstroke will be to produce a "saviour" for mankind. Doesn't it strike you that the world is being led by second-rate leaders? There is a vacuum of personalities. Into that vacuum will step the devil's man, an Antichrist. The spirit who will possess that man is already at work in the world, and affecting people, and contradicting the fact that Christ is both true man and true God.

I recall a little poem:

> "What think ye of Christ?" is the test
> To try both your plan and your scheme.
> You cannot be right in the rest
> Unless you think rightly of him.

It goes straight for the main issue. If they are not right on Christ don't trust them, don't believe another thing. John now writes, "Little children...." Little children are so vulnerable to propaganda. Little children believe what they are told, and then they grow up and find out it is not true. When my children were young they saw an advertisement on television and said, "But that's not true, Daddy." I thank God they were getting discernment concerning propaganda, but wouldn't it be lovely if it was a world where they could believe everything? John the apostle does not want his readers to believe everything but he is not afraid for them. He does not think they will be swept away by false prophets.

Why not? He says three things. First, you have *already* overcome them. They have been in this church, and it says in chapter 2, "They went out from among us". If a false prophet came into your church, you could overcome him. Not by argument, not by knowing your Bible better, not by intellectual superiority, but because he who is in you, the Holy Spirit, is greater than he who is in them. If you have the Holy Spirit in your heart, an evil spirit cannot touch your mind or your heart or your will.

The Holy Spirit has infinitely greater power than Satan. Satan is the spirit of error, the Holy Spirit is the Spirit of truth, and the Spirit of truth overcomes the spirit of error. Indeed the only people that false prophets can get hold of are those without the Holy Spirit. The most clever, intellectual, brilliantly brainy people have been captured by false prophets. Have you ever wondered why highly intelligent people can go into some of the sects and cults? Have you ever wondered why some people with university training can fall for it? The answer is that they don't have the Holy Spirit. One evil spirit is more than a match for an intelligent human being. But the Holy Spirit can defeat one evil spirit and legions of spirits.

Secondly, by way of further proof, you will find that false prophets are popular with unbelievers. They are of the world; the world will listen to them. The fastest growing religious group in the world at the moment is the Jehovah's Witnesses. But you ask them if Jesus is God, test and see what happens. This is the way to see what is going on. Satan has control of the world, and therefore he sends preachers who tickle people's fancy, and they follow them, and they are popular. Why is it that books which attack the Christian faith sell by the million? Don't be surprised.

But the third proof is this: false prophets have no ears for the truth. One of their characteristics is that they won't listen to you. They want you to listen to them but they will not learn from anybody else. They will never sit in the pew and listen to others. They say, "I am inspired, this is the truth and I will not learn from anybody else." Therefore they usually start their own movement gathered around their own personality and their own views. But a true prophet will listen to the Word of God. A true prophet will say, "I can learn from other people preaching to me from the Word of God."

So you can tell the Spirit of truth from the spirit of error. Jesus said "I am the truth". If the devil were honest he would have to say "I am the error", but he would never be that honest. He is the deceiver, the liar, the slanderer – I am quoting Jesus. Therefore the devil says, "I tell the truth; this is from God," and it isn't, and people fall for it. They don't find love, joy and peace, and they don't find forgiveness. They don't come through to the joy of looking for our Lord's return. They don't come through to the joy of heaven because they have been led astray falsely, and they wonder why they are in turmoil and confused.

So how do you tell whether someone is a false prophet? You listen to what comes out of their mouth, and you look at what goes into their ears. Jesus is divine and human, and still divine and human forever now – having come in the flesh and still in the flesh; the divine in our flesh – and whoever denies that is not of God. Whoever confesses that, you can listen to them. The right thing comes out of their mouth. Now look at what goes into their ears. They will not listen to you, nor to anyone else who preaches the Word of God. They are only interested in speaking, not in listening. You can tell – by this we know.

People talk sometimes as if truth and error are things, but they are not things, they are people. There isn't such a thing as truth by itself that you can wrap up in a parcel and say "That's a parcel of truth." There isn't such a "thing" as error. There is only the Spirit of truth and the spirit of error – there is the true Spirit who speaks the truth, and there are evil spirits who speak error. There are only truthful people and dishonest people, and by this you can tell the difference.

Well this is the caution and the warning from John the apostle, "Beloved, little children...." – he is tender towards the congregation. He loves his spiritual children. But he is tough toward error, firm and strong when he is saying don't touch this kind of thing; don't listen to it; don't believe it. Even if the whole world goes after it, don't you fall for it.

Then, from 4:7 onwards, John turns again to love. Once you have found the truth you are capable of love. Truth first, and then love. When you have your faith right, then faith works through love. For the rest of the chapter he is going to say: Beloved, let us love one another, for love is of God. God is love, and whoever loves is born of God and knows God.

This reminds me that the reading at the first service I ever took, the first time I got into a pulpit, was vv. 7–21. My knees were shaking and my family was sitting there, which made it worse. But I read these words, and ever since it has been a favourite passage of mine. In fact my Bible is now broken at just this point, which shows how often I open it to this page.

There can be no doubt what the key word in this passage is. It is the word "love" which occurs twenty-six times in fifteen verses: the love of God. What 1 Corinthians 13 is to the apostle Paul, 1 John 4 is to the apostle John. It is almost poetry. True love bursts out into song and to poetry, and here it is. It is the only passage in the whole Bible to say that God is love, and it says it twice. It is the most sublime statement that has ever been made about the Creator of the whole world. "God is love" – three short, simple words which are so profound that I almost feel I cannot preach on them. They are so deep that I am out of my depth when I read them.

Now the first problem I want to mention is the obvious contrast between the beginning of chapter 4 and the second half of it. John was attacking people using tough language. There are those with sentimental notions of love who would say that he is being very unloving to attack people. But there is a connection between the first part and the second part of the chapter. There is a key word that comes in both parts. It is the word "Spirit". At the end of chapter 3 we are told that God has given us his own Spirit. The Spirit of God is the Spirit of truth and the Spirit of love, and real religion must combine truth and love. A religion that has too much love in it and too little truth becomes too soft, too sentimental. But a religion that has too little love may become too hard.

Real religion is a combination of truth and love, because the Spirit of God is the Spirit of truth and the Spirit of love.

You cannot really love someone until you know the truth about them. It is vital if people are going to get married that they know their partner well enough before marrying, lest they say afterwards, "I had no idea he was like this," or, "I didn't know this was her weakness when we got married." If you are going to have real love it must be based on truth. You can't love God until you know the truth about him. Therefore chapter 4 begins with the truth, and John attacks those who speak untruths about God. But now he goes on to love and he exhorts them, "Beloved, love each other." We recall that incident mentioned earlier in Ephesus: John's constant theme in addressing the church there.

Sixty years before he wrote this letter, he had sat at a table on the last night of his dearest friend's life. He had been leaning his head on Jesus. Between this man John, and the man Jesus, who was the Son of God, there was a closer love than between any of the other disciples and Jesus. He was the disciple whom Jesus loved. On that night Jesus said to all of them, "Little children, I give you a new commandment, that you love each other." It was the only infallible proof to the world that the believers belonged to him – that they would love each other.

John, who loved the Lord very deeply, looked around at the others, one of whom was a rotter and would commit suicide before the night was through. One had been a scribbling little clerk from the customs office who had lined his own pocket from the accounts. Another was a resistance fighter who had hated Romans. Another one was his own brother, nicknamed "a son of thunder" because of his bad temper. Another was impetuous Peter and another was quiet Andrew. John must have thought: What? Love this lot? We're just too different from each other. But on that last night of his life, Jesus made it quite clear that it is impossible to love Jesus if you don't love Christians – absolutely out of the question. For the first time and for the last time Jesus made it clear that you cannot divorce love of the Father from love of the brother. You cannot possibly love God if you don't love his people. You cannot possibly know what the Father's love is if you don't love your brother. The two are one, and you cannot drive a wedge between them. So that love is something that flows from the Father to our brother, and it has got to flow or it doesn't shine in us.

Now John is first of all going to talk about God's love for a few verses and then about our love. In vv. 7–12 he is talking about God. The word "God" comes fourteen times in just these six verses. That is where love begins; it doesn't begin with me, it begins with him. Love doesn't flow from me first; it flows from him first to me. It is not that we have loved him, it is that he has loved us. That is where true religion begins.

We consider now the simple fact that by nature I am quite incapable of the kind of love talked of here. I could love my wife without knowing God. I could love my friends and relatives, or at least some of them. I could love my country to a degree, but I cannot love like God loves unless I know God. He who loves is born of God and knows God. He who does not love does not know God. It is as simple as that. When I say "love" I am not meaning what we mean when we talk of a couple loving each other and getting married. What am I talking about? I'm talking about this peculiar love that God has for people and it is different from any other love. There are three stages by which this love reaches me: the heavenly stage, the historical stage and the human stage. It begins in heaven in the very personality of God. Here we have these amazing words "God is love". Now that is an astonishing statement. To say God is love is to say what he *is*. I can't even begin to plumb the depths of that statement, "God is love". No other religion in the world has ever said that. You can read every other book. You can read the Vedas, you can read the Koran, you can read anything you like, but no other religion says those three words "God is love". What do they mean?

First of all, it means that *love really does exist*. People cry for it, people long for it, people sing about it; people grope after it. Everybody is looking for love. Deep down, everybody needs to be loved and everybody is asking, "Is there such a thing as real love? Does it exist anywhere? Is there any such thing as perfect love?" Well, if you only look at the level of human relationships, there is no such thing as perfect love. If that is the only place you have got to look, you will be eternally frustrated and disappointed. But as soon as I look at God, I know that love really does exist – real love.

If I say "God loved the world" that is one thing, but that means there was a world to love. However, if I say "God is love" – before there was a world, before there was anybody to love – God was love; love existed before anything else existed. It will exist after everything is gone. Love is there. It is the most real thing in the universe because it always was there. God is love and if people say, "I don't believe that there's such a thing as love," then they are saying, "I don't believe that there is such a person as God, and I don't believe that God is love."

Here is the second thing I see in this: God must be more than one person. You couldn't say "God is love" if God was only one person by himself, because love cannot exist with one person only. One man on a desert island cannot love. You have got to have someone else to love. Then how could God be love before there was any world and before there were any people? The answer is that from all eternity God has been plural, not singular. In the very beginning of the Bible in the Hebrew language, it says: "In the beginning Gods [the word is plural, actually triple] created the heaven and the earth," and, "Gods said, 'let *us* make man in *our* own image.'" This is why Christians believe in the Trinity – because they believe God is love. If you only believe that God is one person then you cannot say that God is love – because who was he loving before there was anybody to love? From all eternity the Father loved the Son, and the Son loved the Father, and the Father and Son loved the Spirit, and the Spirit loved the Father and Son – God is love.

The third thing is this: if God is love then that is why he loves me. Isn't that tremendous? He doesn't love me because I am lovable. He doesn't love me because I am nice to know. He doesn't love me because I am lovely. He loves me because he is love – that is the reason. Why does God love the Jews? Not many other people do. They may admire them, they may respect them, they make think they are brilliant commercial businessmen, that they have great gifts. Why does God love such people? It is written into the Old Testament. God says, "Why do you think I love you, my people Israel? Because you are greater than any other people on the face of the earth? No, I love you because I love you." That is all.

Why does God love any of us? Why should God love you? I am sure you could ask the same question of me. Why on earth does God love him? Because God is love. It is the only reason, there is no other explanation. This is his love, and it is in his personality. It is not just something that he *does*; it is something that he *is*.

The love of God is first a heavenly thing that was always there in his personality, but how then did it ever get to us? How did anybody discover that God is love? When God was just loving himself up there, how did anybody know? The answer is that the heavenly love came into time and space and invaded our world, and was manifested among us, and became something historical, something that you can date,

something that split history in two, something that is fact—
and he sent his own and only Son.

The word "sent" is the same as the word "apostle", the
same as our word "missionary", which is the same as our
word "missile". Therefore what I am going to say is this:
the love of God created a mission control centre in heaven,
and sent his Son as a missile, a mission, a missionary to this
planet. We are so bemused and excited with missions and
missiles being sent out when we should be terribly excited
about the missions sent in. God sent his own Son – why?
Because it was a matter of life and death, because people
on earth were dying and would go on dying spiritually,
physically, mentally, emotionally and morally – in every
way people on earth were dying. God loved us and he sent
his own Son into the world that we might live through him.

Why were we dying? The answer is quite simple: it was
our own fault. It was because of what we were doing. It
was because of our sins. It was because of our refusal to go
his way, our refusal to let him run our lives, and we were
killing ourselves because of this. Therefore, in some amazing
way God had to find a way of dealing with our sins without
becoming immoral himself. If God had let us off he would
have become an immoral God. If he had just said, "OK, we'll
forgive and forget" then that would have been an immoral
act, and he couldn't do it. How could he get round it? He
sent his Son to be the propitiation for our sins. At the cross,
and only at the cross, people saw that God is love, that he
sent his own Son to die for us.

John adds something at this point. The difference
between Christianity and every other religion is this:
*Christianity starts with God's love for us, and not our love
for God.* Christianity doesn't say, "This is the way to find
God." Christianity says: "God has come looking for you."
Christianity doesn't start with man's initiative but with

God's, and every other religion says, "These are the steps to climb up to God: fast, pray, give, make a pilgrimage" or whatever, and climb up to God. Christianity says that God climbed down to you, and he will meet you where you are.

So herein is love: not that we loved God – it is not what you do for God that makes you a Christian, it is what God does for you. Yet there are people in churches in England who think it is the other way round. If you ask them, "Are you a Christian?" they would say, "Well, I'm trying to be." You say, "What on earth do you mean by that remark?" They say, "Well, I go to church and I do this, that and the other. And I try to live right and I try to help people," and it's all them, it's all on this side. It's all what I do for God. Herein is love: not what we do for God, not that we love him, but that he loved us.

The heavenly love became historical love. It was there BC/AD; it was right there in the middle of history, planted firmly into a rock called Golgotha. But even that is two thousand years ago, so how does it get to me? Not through our senses, for no man has ever seen God, but through the fellowship of those who love each other. If you want to know where to find God to be real, go to a fellowship where Christians love each other and you will know that God is real. No man has ever seen God at any time, but if we abide in God, if we love one another, then we know God is real, he abides among us.

We see through a mirror dimly. We can only see the reflection of God's love, but you see it in the fellowship of those who love one another. I know of nothing that convinces people of the reality of God like getting in among a group of Christians who love each other.

Now we turn to human love, our love. How can we be sure that God abides in us and we in him? The answer is that he has given us of his Spirit. You don't have to imitate God's love; all you need do is let it flow. God's love is shed abroad in our hearts through the Holy Spirit given to us. You don't have to *try* to love like God, all you need do is let God's love flow through.

Of course if there is a blockage then God's love can't even flow in, because it has got to flow *through*. If we are loving our brethren then God's love is flowing through us. It is not *our* love, it never will be *our* love, it will always be God's love flowing through. How do you know when you have got the Spirit? How do you know that this is God's love when you are loving someone? Three signs: it will be a faithful love, it will be a fearless love and it will be a fraternal love. None of these kinds of love do you find in the unbeliever, only in the brother Christian.

First of all, loving is related to believing. It is full of faith. It will be a testifying love. If you really have the love of God in you then you will talk about Jesus. You will testify that God sent him to be the Saviour of the world. You will confess him before other people. Is God's love in you? Then your mouth will glorify the Lord Jesus. If I love him, I talk. And what do I say? I will tell people he is sent by the Father. I will tell them he is the Saviour. I will tell them that he is God's own Son. I will say it is because of Jesus that I know and believe the love that God has for me and the love that he has in himself. This, then, is the first test of love. When did you last meet an unbeliever who talked to others about Jesus? They may have a human love for people, but they don't have God's love, they don't testify, they don't confess.

The second test concerns fear. On the whole, people pass through four stages of fear in relation to love. There is the stage when they have neither fear of God nor love for God. They don't really know him; therefore they neither fear him nor know him. Stage number two: they come to believe that God is Judge, and that one day they will stand before him and their lives will be an open book in his sight, and they fear

127

him but they don't love him – but the fear is the beginning of wisdom. Stage number three: they begin to love him so the fear gets less and the love grows greater. Stage number four: perfect love casts out fear. Everyone will stand before God, whether they believe it or not, whether they like it or not. There is only one thing that can prepare you for that day with confidence, and it is that you love God; that you can stand before him in that day and say with Simon Peter, "You know everything, you know that I love you" – that's all.

The third test is fraternal love. In 4:19 John wrote: we love him because he first loved us. The proof of God's love is this: if you have got it, you give it. If you have received it, you pass it on. If it is coming into your life it has got to go out. If it is not going out then it has not come in. If you don't love others you haven't realised that he has first loved you.

John just calls certain people liars. If you say you love God and yet you obviously don't love your Christian brother, you are a liar, you are not speaking the truth. If I don't love my Christian brother, I don't love my Father. It is a test of love. If God's love is in me, then as soon as I meet another Christian I see God's image there, I see one of my family there. If you can't love your brother whom you can see, how can you love your Father? You can't. There is God's image standing before you and it is much easier to love someone you can see than someone you can't see. How can you say you love God if you don't love God in your brother? It is logical and it is the truth. So love casts out hatred as well as fear. Nobody is ever going to tell you that you will like everybody you meet. By nature we like some and we don't like others. But God's love is not a "liking" love. Wouldn't it be terrible if the Bible said "God likes us"? Love doesn't care whether it likes a person or it doesn't like them, it loves them. God loved the world because he is love. If God's love is in us we no longer talk about liking people and disliking them. We love them because God's love is in us. That is the proof that we have got his love.

In 4:7 we have "love one another" and in 4:21 we have come right around to it again: "This is the commandment, that he who loves God loves his brother also." It is not an optional extra that you should get to know and love your fellow Christian, it is a commandment, a must.

God is love and God's people are to love one another. I finish by underlining what I pointed out earlier: that nowhere does the Bible tell you to imitate God's love; nowhere does it say that you have got to love like God loves you. What it does teach is this: open up your life in two directions – open it to God, open it to your brother, and let the love flow. That is all. We don't need to do anything other than that to abide in God and have God abiding in us.

FAITH BASED ON FACT

Read 1 John 5:1–12

There is an old proverb that says, "Hurt my child and you hurt me." This is true of every ordinary, normal earthly family. If you hurt the child you hurt the parent. We have seen in 1 John that the same applies to the heavenly family. If you hurt a child of God you hurt God. You cannot say "I love God" if you hate his children. You are a liar; it's not true. If you love God you love his child. You cannot divorce God from his children. Many people try, many say they can, and they either say that they love God's children or that they love God, but you can't have one without the other.

1 John 5:1–5 develops this acid test of our relationship. If you have been born of God you have been born into a family. You not only have a heavenly Father, you have earthly brothers and sisters. Your relationship to them is involved in your relationship to him. Before we apply this test more fully we have to answer a question: if it is a test of my love for God that I love his children, *who are they*? Some people would answer straight away, "Well, every human being on earth is a child of God and the proof that you love God will be that you love everybody on earth." But the Bible does not teach that. All people are not the children of God. We have seen this again and again in this letter already – that the world is made up of two families, not one: the children of God and the children of the world. These are two families who don't get on with each other and never will. The Bible makes no bones about this – there always will be tension and division between the children of God and the children of the world.

Sometimes the tension will be less, sometimes more. This dividing line between the two families runs through many earthly families. It runs right through every village, every town, every city. It can even run through a congregation in a church.

Who are these children of his, loving whom will prove that I love him? It is vital that I should know that before I apply the test, because only then can I say, "Do I love these people?" The answer is *faith*. The key word in this whole section is "believe" or "faith". This is what marks the children of God from everybody else. The children of God have faith, but what kind of a faith? It is not a vague and general faith, that there is somebody up there who looks after me, or something, somewhere. That is not the kind of faith that makes a child of God. What, then, is the faith that makes a person a child of God? *Everyone who believes that Jesus is the Christ is a child of God.* You notice it doesn't say that everyone who believes that there is a God is a child of God. Many people believe that there is a God. They have all kinds of ideas as to what he is like, and often they are very vague about it, but most people I meet say, "Oh yes, I believe in God, I don't want you to think I don't." But that doesn't make them a child of God. Faith in God never made anybody a child of God – faith in *Jesus* is what makes you a child of the heavenly Father.

On the last night before he died, Jesus said to his disciples, "You believe in God, believe also in me." I paraphrase: if you are ever going to get to heaven you will need to believe in me as well as God. Christian belief is not belief in God, it is belief in Jesus, and through him belief in God. It is the only way to become a child of God. There is no shortcut and therefore I say to any who will listen to me: "You may believe in God, it doesn't make you a child of God, and it won't get you to heaven. Believe in Jesus and the gates of heaven fling wide open to you. You are now part of the family. You have become a brother or a sister to me, and a child to my heavenly Father."

But it is not just to believe in Jesus in the sense that Jesus was a great man, a great teacher, a great healer, a man who went about doing good, and a man who lived the only perfect life that has ever been lived. I have never met anyone who would read the life of Jesus and then refuse to say to me afterwards, "That's the greatest life I've ever read about, even though it was so short, even though I only know three years of it." But that doesn't make you a child of God. It is *everyone who believes that Jesus is the Christ*. Every word of that sentence is absolutely fundamental to Christian faith. It is only if you believe all those words *Jesus is the Christ* that you have become a child of God.

Let me say a little about each word. Firstly, the word "Jesus". That is a name given to a little baby born in Bethlehem who grew up and lived on this earth for thirty-three years – a real human being whom people touched and ate with, and walked and talked with. The first step in Christian belief is to believe that there was a person, a human being called Jesus who lived at a particular time in a particular place. You may have been to that place and even looked at the shores where he went fishing with his disciples, but you and I were not there at the time. We may have looked at the roads where he went walking with his disciples and seen the hill where they murdered him – it is as real as that. That is the first step. You will never get anywhere in seeking to become a child of God until you start with the human being called Jesus.

Now for the second word in this phrase: "is". Here is something that you cannot say about any other human being. Julius Caesar *was*; Jesus *is*. You are not a believer until you say "is". Even if you think there was a great man called Jesus, a wonderful personality who did more for other people than anybody else in the whole wide world – you may believe all that, but if you believe that he is dead today, you are not a child of God yet. So Jesus *is* – and in that little two-letter word is the good news of Christianity – that Jesus, even though they murdered him, is alive *now*. It is not what he "was" that makes you a believer, it is what he "is". *Right now, Jesus is*. If you believe that, you are on your way to being a believer.

Let us now look at the word "Christ". What does that mean? Two things. It means that in Jesus, this human being, you find two things that you will not find in anyone else: first *divinity* and second *deliverance*. The word "Christ" means both these things. It means first that Jesus is God. This human being is divine. If you want to know what God is like, meet Jesus. If you want to know what all of God is like, meet all of Jesus. "For the fullness of the Godhead dwells in him bodily," says the Bible. *Deliverance* – because this human being is God, he can do more for you than anybody else can do for you: he can deliver you from sickness, he can deliver you from sin, he can deliver you from death, he can deliver you from fear, he can deliver you from enslavement to bad habits. He can deliver you from all these things. Now you understand what the word "the" means. If it was "Jesus was *a* Christ" it assumes that there are others who can do all this for you. But if I say he is *the* Christ then I mean he is the *only* one. Nobody else can do this for me. Nobody else can save me and deliver me from those things which blight my life and my character. Therefore you are a child of God if you really believe that the human being Jesus is the Christ, God, the deliverer, the Saviour.

You notice it doesn't say "everyone who *says* that" – you can say it without believing it. You can teach a parrot to say these words. I have never heard it done but I once came across a budgerigar that could sing hymns! There it was and it sang hymns, and it sang them as well as some of my congregation, but it didn't make that budgie a Christian; that budgie isn't a child of God. It is not *saying* these things that makes you a child of God. Everyone who *believes* this is a child of God. If you want to know who the children of God are, find out who believes that Jesus is the Christ, and you have found a child of God.

Having defined a child of God we can now apply the test. Do you love the people who believe this? If so, then you love the Father. If you love everybody you meet who really believes this, then you do love God, it is the proof. You love the children, so you love the Father. Nothing could be simpler and I want to be with the family, I can't stay away from them. So ask yourself, "When I meet someone who believes that Jesus is the Christ, do I love them?" If I don't then I should question whether I love God, because the two things belong together.

Now that covers our *fellowship* and quite frankly it gives the absolute lie to the old adage, "I can be a Christian without going to church." You hear it wherever you go, but it is rubbish and self-delusion. How can someone say they love God if they ignore his children? How can someone say that they are a child of God if they have nothing to do with his family? How can they possibly even think it? Ignore his family and you are ignoring God; hurt his family and you are hurting God; mock his family and you are mocking God; criticise his family and you are criticising God; love his family and you are loving God. But how then do we know whether we love his children? I meet his children. They tell me – and I know that they believe – that Jesus is the Christ. How do I know if I love them? Is it because I have a nice sort of bubbly feeling inside as soon as I meet them? Christianity is not really terribly concerned with your feelings. It is lovely to have them, and from time to time God gives us such feelings that we don't know whether we are in heaven or on earth. But it doesn't really matter whether we have those or not – that is not a test of whether we love his children. What is the test? John gives us two simple practical tests as to whether we love the children of God. The first is this: you can prove that you love the children of God if you love God. Now that sounds strange! The proof that you love God is that you love his children, and the proof that you love his children is that you love God. Is John taking us around in circles? Where does this argument begin and end? The answer is that it doesn't begin and end anywhere, it is like a circle. In other words, each thing proves the other. If you want proof that you love God it will be that you love his children. If you want proof that you love his children it will be that you love God. Love flows from the Father through you to the brother, and back to the Father.

Think of a couple who fall in love. People may say, "I just don't know what they see in each other." Of course they don't, because they are not in that circle of love. But those two who are in it do know because love is flowing. They know they love each other. If you say "Prove it to me," the girl would say, "He loves me," and the boy would say, "She loves me." You might say, "That's no proof to me." Of course it isn't, you can't prove love to anyone who is outside it. But when you are inside the circle the love flows both ways, and each proves the other. How do I know that I love the Father? I love the brother. How do I know that I love the brother? I love God. The two confirm each other and love flows.

Somebody will say, "Well that's not enough to test whether I really love." Now John adds one more thing. *The proof that you love God is that you keep his commandments.* Do you notice that it has nothing to do with your feelings? The proof is practical. If you want to know if you are loving your Father and your brother – do you keep the commandments?

The Ten Commandments are a good example. Five are concerned with loving God and five with loving your fellow men and women. Do you keep them? There is something very important here. John says that to the one who loves God the commandments are not irksome, not burdensome, not irritating. Now I am going to prove that to you in a rather simple but delightful way. I want you to imagine for a moment that it is not God giving you the Ten Commandments but a human being with whom you are deeply in love. Let me try and imagine for myself. Here is this lovely young lady – I am thinking of my wife at the moment, but trying to be impersonal. She says to me, "Now then, here's my commandment number one: thou shalt have no other girls before me." Right, what do I say? If I love this girl, do you think that is an irksome commandment? Do you think that's a tough one? Of course it isn't. Now if I didn't love her, if she was a nagging person whom I didn't love at all, that commandment would irritate me tremendously. Now do you see the difference?

When God says, "You shall have no other gods before me" – if you love God, that is a lovely commandment. Who wants another god? But if you don't love God that is not a very nice commandment, it is irksome. Let's go a little further. Supposing the girl with whom I am in love says to me, "You shall spend one day in seven with me." I say, "May I? A whole day in seven? I would spend seven if I could" – but then, if I didn't love her, if I didn't like her one bit, what an irksome commandment it would be. Again, can you see the difference?

If your girl said to you, "You shall not steal from me," you would say, "Don't talk silly. I love you. I want to give you things. I don't want to take things from you."

People who don't love God say, "These Ten Commandments, I don't like them one bit, they are old-fashioned, out of date, negative – 'Thou shalt not', just spoiling my fun." Doesn't that prove they don't love God? But when you love God they are not burdensome. "My yoke is easy," said Jesus, "My burden is light." They are the way to show your love.

Here is the test. Go through the Ten Commandments: God is telling you how to express love. If you don't like the commandments, if you rebel against them, if you hate them, if you are irritated by them, then you don't love God. But if you love God you will find that you keep his commandments, and they are not burdensome.

The next point is what the psychologists call "the expulsive power of a new affection". They can call it what they like! I will tell you what the Bible calls it: *overcoming the world*. The world does not love God, and therefore the world does not keep his commandments. Many people find it irksome to think of spending Sunday in God's presence, they find it irksome to have all these "thou shalt nots", and they say: "I want to be free, I want to break the commandments." That is the world that we have to go on living in after we have become Christians. But here is the victory that overcomes the world. No longer are you subject to the pressure of a society that makes you conform to a loveless, commandment-breaking world.

A person who is spiritually dead must go with the world. They must go with not loving God; they must go with breaking his commandments. They must go with this irksome, burdensome attitude to God's law. But a person who has been born of God overcomes the world and loves to do what God has commanded. This is how you may know.

Now all this is so sensible, so real, so down to earth and practical. The amazing thing is that the unbeliever can read verses 1–5 and doesn't know what it is all about. He can't even see it; he can't even understand simple words like this. What is it that gives us the power to swim against the stream? What is it that gives us the power not to conform to a loveless society? When I say "loveless" I mean primarily that it doesn't love God. You will find human love in society but not divine love. What is it? It is our *faith*.

Some let society shape them by conforming, and some let society shape them by not conforming. The desire to be free is a desire to be free to break the commandments, to break the law, to break the order of God in society, as well as in conscience. So our society is made up at the moment of the rebels and the respectable – those who have conformed to society and those who have rebelled against it, and they are both running with the stream, whether they know it or not, in different ways.

Real freedom – and only the believer has this – is to be free to keep the commandments. Nobody else is free to keep the commandments. The real freedom God wants us to have is to be free to love him, to honour his name, to honour our parents, to be free not to kill, to be free not to steal, to be free not to commit adultery, to be free not to lie about others, free not to covet and free not to want everything you see. This freedom is there for the child of God.

But many today want a different sort of freedom: they want to be free to be dirty in a disinfected world, free to be rebels in a respectable world, and free to be promiscuous in a prim world, but that is not freedom, it is slavery – sheer bondage. Real freedom is freedom not to be respectable, but freedom to love God. Real freedom is not to be religious but freedom to be Christian. Real freedom is to be free to keep the commandments and you never will be free to keep them until you love God and believe that Jesus is the Christ.

In vv. 1–5 we began with everyone who believes and we finish with a rhetorical question: "Who is it that overcomes the world?" The answer: "*Only he who believes that Jesus is the Son of God*." If you search for one person in your town who runs against the stream and keeps the commandments of God and doesn't find them burdensome but also doesn't believe that Jesus is the Son of God, you are going to be looking a very long time!

What is faith based on? Is it solid? Having written in vv. 1–5 of how faith introduces us to love, which leads to obedience, John now tells us what faith is based on. It is based on two facts: real life in Jesus; real life in us. So John begins with the life of Christ. When you are not present at events, the only way in which you can come to believe them to be real and true is on the testimony of witnesses. Every law court is based on the same principle, and every case that I have ever sat through is based on such evidence. If you are not prepared to believe a thing because you were not there, then you never will get anywhere in the Christian faith because you just weren't there when Christ came.

Let me give you a modern illustration. I was reading of a wonderful case where Jesus raised a woman from the dead. As he did in the days of his flesh, he has done it again. I have heard of a number of such cases in modern times. I wasn't there, but I believe it. Why do I believe it? Is it because I'll believe anything? No, I believe because of the witnesses who testified to it. Because I am prepared to accept that truth can come to me, the truth of events, even though I wasn't there – through the testimony of witnesses who were. We would accept that in a law court, so why will we not accept it in a church? That is what John is going to point out: you will accept the testimony of men, why will you not accept the testimony of God? There are witnesses to the facts that life – real life – was in Jesus, God's Son.

John now starts talking about water and blood. What on earth does he mean? Water is real, blood is real, and they are both liquids in my body. When Jesus was on the cross a soldier pierced his side with a spear and it says that from the wound there flowed water and blood. It was real. What is he talking about? He is talking about two historical events in which God testified to his Son. There was a day when Jesus was baptised in water. I have been to the very spot and I have baptised someone there. Jesus was baptised in water; he came by water. What happened at that time? It sounded like thunder, and a voice from heaven said, "You are my beloved Son, in whom I am well pleased." God testified and there were people there who heard it and who wrote it down and you have got their testimony. Whose testimony are you going to believe? When Jesus came by water in baptism, *God* testified.

God spoke again just before Jesus died, and the people said that it thundered. But some heard the words, and God again said, "This is my Son". He came by blood and he really died, and the blood really flowed. It was real, red human blood. These events were real – so whose testimony are you going to believe? Those who say that he is not the Son of God, that he is not divine, not the Christ – or God, who says he is? It's the word of God against the words of men. Whose testimony do you accept?

There is a third witness – the Spirit. Jesus was baptised in water, and God testified: "This is my Son". Jesus, as he put it in his own words, had another baptism to be baptised with, to be baptised in blood. God said "This is my Son" and raised him from the dead to prove it. Seven weeks later there was another baptism. This time Jesus was the baptiser and baptised men and women in the Holy Spirit, and this again was proof that God was testifying to his Son. God has poured out this which you see and hear. It is God who is saying "Jesus is my Son" and these three baptisms of water, blood and the Spirit are God's testimony.

Of these three, I was not present at the water baptism of Jesus, so I have to take that on the testimony of witnesses. I was not present at his baptism in blood, so I have to take that on the testimony of witnesses. But the testimony of the baptism in the Spirit is going on today, which is why John says the Spirit is the third witness. Whenever someone is baptised in the Holy Spirit today, that is God testifying that Jesus is his Son. Whose testimony are you going to accept? All through the ages there have been millions of people filled with the Holy Spirit testifying to the Son of God.

Here is the choice. You would accept the testimony of three witnesses in a court who agreed, wouldn't you? You would say, "That's what must have happened." Why then will people not accept the witnesses of God? There are these three: the water, the blood, and the Spirit. These are historical events and the evidence for them is far stronger and far greater than for any other event we take as historical. Why then do people not agree? Whoever does not agree is calling God a liar. If I meet a man who says he doesn't believe what is written in the Bible, then I have that book's authority to call him a liar because he is calling God a liar. It is God's Word against men. Did the things recorded there happen? This is God's testimony through his witnesses.

Then to say "I don't believe it" is to say: "God, you're a liar; you're a false witness," and that to me would be the ultimate blasphemy and the ultimate lie.

But for the Christian, what happens? They believe the external evidence, and now to that is added the internal evidence: the believer now has the testimony in himself. It must irritate unbelievers that believers are so sure. I used to be irritated when I was an unbeliever. I remember as a student at college there was a Christian, only one in our whole year, and he irritated me enormously. He was so jolly sure of what he believed. I said as most unbelievers

do, "Nobody can be as sure as that, you're just conceited."
He was *so* sure!

Then there came a day when I believed the evidence and
the testimony and the witnesses of God to the truth. Do you
know what I found? I found that an extra testimony in myself
said: you were right to believe them because now you have
the testimony inside. It is not just that Christians have the
evidence, they have it in themselves. Why do I believe that
Jesus is alive? Because all the evidence points that way?
Partly, but only partly. I will tell you why I really believe
it: because the Spirit of Jesus is in my heart and I have got
the evidence inside.

This is the testimony that God has given us: eternal life.
Eternal life means life of a new quality and life of a new
quantity – both. Eternal life means a new *quality* of life.
You never knew that you could live like this before. You
never knew that life could be so alive. Real life is also a
new *quantity* because it will go on forever. You know that
you have something now that not even death can take away
from you. You have the testimony in yourself.

Therefore we finish up with this simple, logical, clear
alternative: if you have got the Son of God you have got
life; if you haven't got the Son of God you are not alive.
You may exist, and it may be years before the undertaker
comes for you, but you are not alive.

Real, true, eternal life is this: to know God and to know
Jesus whom he has sent. Anybody else may not know it
but they are dead and they are heading for physical death
because they have already got spiritual death in them – life
is just death, and that is all there is for them to look forward
to. But if you have the Son you have got life, and this life is
in God's Son. You can't have eternal life without Jesus – the
two go together.

This is my faith, and it is not based on fancy or fiction or feeling. It is based, firstly, on the fact that real life is in the Son; and, secondly, that real life is in me when his Spirit is in me. So I have the external evidence of Jesus' life and the internal evidence of *my* life. Once again, those who know this life need no more proof, no more facts and no more persuasion. You will find that they have an unshakeable assurance of faith. His life; my life – because his life is now mine – that is the Christian truth. Whoever has the Son has life, and he that has not the Son has not life. Faith based on fact leads to love of the Father and the brother, and that is proved by obedience and keeping the commandments.

KNOWING

Read 1 John 5:13–21

We live in an age of agnosticism, and "agnostic" simply means "don't know". Opinion polls have a category for the "don't knows", the agnostics, and the number in that category gets bigger when you get on to religious questions. I meet an increasingly large number of people who, if you ask them whether there is a God or not, say that they don't know. If you ask them whether there is life after death or not, they don't know. If you ask them whether miracles happen today they don't know.

This is the age in which we live, and not only do people say "I don't know", they often go on to say, "And you can't know." That is agnosticism in its strongest form – to say that you can't be sure, that you can't know whether there is a God, that you can't know whether you are going to heaven, that this is beyond the reach of our minds. It is a refreshing change to turn from the agnosticism of our newspapers and magazines telling us they don't know and they can't know, and turn to a book like 1 John that says repeatedly (seven times in this passage) "we know". John wrote this letter to those who believe, that they may *know*.

It is not enough just to believe. Christians are those who *know* as well as believe. They are sure, and we are going to look at what they are sure of, and we are going to ask how you get to be sure of these things. But when John says, "I write to you who believe, that you may know," that means two things to me. Firstly, that a believer can be unsure. You can believe without knowing. Secondly, a believer can be sure and ought to be. Take the first: it is possible for a Christian to have doubts – for someone who has believed in the Lord Jesus to have real heart-searching, to wonder from time to time whether they are a Christian. So John writes to those believers who may have doubts.

Now you notice what the doubt is: *they don't have doubts about Christ, they have doubts about themselves*. John writes to people who believe in the name of the Son of God. So they are sure of that, but he writes "so that you may know you have eternal life". He wants them to be sure of that.

The Lord doesn't want any one of his children to doubt that. I don't want my children ever to doubt that they are my children; I don't want them to have that uncertainty. I want them to be sure that they belong to me and I belong to them. I don't want them ever to feel that my love for them could stop. I don't want them ever to feel that I would let them go, and my heavenly Father doesn't want his children ever to feel that either. Why? Because unless you are sure, unless you know you have eternal life, you lose boldness in speaking, and your prayer life suffers, as well as preaching and your testimony. The person who knows they have eternal life has confidence in talking to God and confidence in talking to other people. Therefore John writes, "... to you who believe in the name of the Son of God *so that you may know you have eternal life*."

The whole of this little letter is giving us certain practical tests as to how we may know that we have eternal life. We have seen that the tests are just three: belief; behaviour; brotherhood. How do you know that you have eternal life? You believe that Jesus Christ is the Son of God; you keep the commandments; you love your Christian brothers and sisters. Every person may be quite sure that they have eternal life by just applying the three tests. If you are not sure then I beg you to seek to be sure, so that you may not only believe but may know. At this point John uses the word "we" ("this is the confidence we have"), and he speaks for himself, for all the apostles and the others who have walked with the Lord for so long. This aged apostle, the last living disciple to have walked with Jesus in the flesh, will die soon after he has written this letter. He can write of things of which he is confident, and he wants his readers to be sure too. There are four things he knows about which he writes to you in order that you may know too.

What are they? First, we know that our intercession is answered. That is the apostle John's confidence: "Whatever we ask, according to his will, he hears us and he gives us what we ask." To think that you can know that what you ask for from God you have got – that is confidence. The unbeliever does not have that confidence. He prays as a last resort and hopes that something might happen but he doesn't know it will. Even many Christians don't have that assurance. They believe and they pray but they don't know that they are going to get an answer. When you really have this confidence of being sure of eternal life, you can ask for something and know you have got it before you get it.

Let us look at this carefully. There are two things you will be sure of when you know you have eternal life. The first is that God hears your prayer. Sometimes prayer is like talking into a telephone without being aware of anyone at the other end of the line – you are just talking. But when you know that you have eternal life you are sure that he hears; there is an ear listening. As soon as you say "Father" you have all of his attention. You know, and that is a wonderful thing. But not only do you know that he hears you, also you know that he is going to give you what you ask for, and this is almost breathtaking. You may now be thinking, "Well, I asked him for something and I didn't get it." There are certain conditions and here is the first: "...if you ask anything *according to his will.*" What does that mean? It means that it must not be a prayer according to your desire. It must be what he would want and what he does want. If it is what he wants, you can be absolutely sure you will get it. Therefore, when you pray for it you have got it, and you can thank him before it comes along. You could put it this way: prayer is not a way of getting God to do our will, nor is it a way of getting us to do his will, it is a way of getting him to do his will. If I say you can only have what is according to his will, someone will say, "Oh well, what's the point of asking? What's the point of praying? If he's willed it, it'll happen." It won't. God has so arranged affairs that many things will not happen unless we ask, even if it is his will. It is his will that all men shall be saved, but that will not happen unless we ask. But if we ask according to his will, it is done and we can know.

If you think back over the prayers that you asked that were never answered, be utterly honest with yourself and ask: did I stop to find out if this was my will or his? Did I ask whether this was the earnest desire of my heart, or the earnest desire of his? Look back over your prayer life and consider that very carefully. This confidence in prayer is a wonderful thing.

Thinking again of that little lady I used to go to visit who never asked a prayer without thanking God for the answer before she got off her knees – the result was she didn't have a failure; she was amazing. But then she had walked with the Lord so closely that she understood his will. She didn't ask for a thing if it wasn't according to his will. But you may say, "Well, it would have happened if she hadn't asked." No it wouldn't. God was waiting for some soul on earth just to say, "Please..." and then it came.

John is particularly concerned with prayer that is not for me but for my Christian brother who is going wrong. This is the bigger thing in prayer. If you love your brother or sister, you pray for them. The proof that you love someone is that you will remember them before the throne of grace and you pray for them. There is a prayer for an erring brother that will be answered by God, that is according to his will. You can be absolutely sure that it is the will of God that an erring brother be brought back, and that is a prayer you can be confident he will answer. Maybe not within twenty-four hours, but he will answer it, and you go on praying until he does, sure that he will. In fact it says if you see a brother committing a sin then you should talk about it not to people but to God. Claim this verse and say, "God, I know this is your will. I pray that you will answer my prayer for my brother."

According to v. 16, God will answer the prayer and give life for that brother to you to give to him. In other words, he will give you the answer to that prayer. He will give you what the brother needs, and that is a wonderful pattern of prayer. If I had not prayed, that brother would have gone on doing wrong and the situation would have got worse and worse, but because I pray God gives me life for him.

Now comes a rather puzzling part of this little letter, which I don't want you to get obsessed with. But there is one situation in which praying for a sinning brother Christian will not in fact do anything – when it is not the will of God to bring that brother back. We have the phrase, and a very funny phrase it is now: "mortal sin". If it is mortal sin we are not to pray because it will do no good, even with an erring brother. What is this sin? I am afraid some people have got so worked up about this that they have made lists: venial and mortal or deadly sins. A list was worked out in the Middle Ages of seven deadly sins, which are so mortal that it is no use praying for someone who is doing them: pride, sloth, lust.... When you read them through, that pretty well cuts all of us out of the picture. I think that list is a wrong list; it doesn't come out of the Bible, and I am not going to teach that kind of list to you. The seven deadly sins as I understand it can all be forgiven and are worth praying about. So if you meet a proud brother or a lazy brother, pray for him, it might get him back – it will get him back, it is the will of the Lord.

But what is this mortal sin? Some have thought it was the unforgivable sin that Jesus mentioned in Mark 3, where he talks about people who say that the work of the Holy Spirit is the work of the devil, and the work of the devil is the work of the Lord, who get themselves so brainwashed that they have convinced themselves that good is evil and evil is good, and black is white and white is black. That is an unforgivable sin because a man who has brainwashed himself to believe that can't even see what needs forgiving. I have only met once or twice in many years of ministry anyone who was even getting within a hundred miles of doing that, but it is a possibility and we must remember it. But I don't think that's what is meant here because that is the sin of an unbeliever. You don't find a believer doing that, and this is a brother. Some have thought it is the sin mentioned in Hebrews 6 of apostasy – a man who has been enlightened, who has tasted the powers of the age to come, and then has deliberately, knowing what he is doing, turned his back on Christ and denied that Jesus is the Saviour, and utterly blasphemed and absolutely renounced Christ as the Son of God. We are told in Hebrews 6 that you cannot do anything more for a man like that because he has cut himself off from the only person who can help him: Christ. Is that what is meant? No, I don't think I have come across believers doing that.

What then is the mortal sin mentioned? It is always a good principle to look elsewhere in the Bible. There are three cases in the New Testament of Christians sinning when the sin is so dangerous and so wrong, so I mention them here. Ananias and Sapphira gave a lump sum of money to the church for the work of God and they said, "We've sold our property and here are the whole proceeds." Everybody was inspired by this tremendous gift and thought what a great gift it was, and it was a lie. They had not given all that they had got for their property; they had kept some of it back and they had taken glory to themselves for giving it all. Simon Peter recognised that their sin was so dangerous that these two were better dead than going on living in the church. He said to those two, "They'll carry you out of this building and bury you," and they did.

The second occasion mentioned in scripture is in 1 Corinthians 5 where a Christian brother in the fellowship was living in an incestuous relationship with his mother. The whole of Corinth knew about it, and the whole of Corinth said "Even pagans don't do that." Paul wrote: "You are to deliver this man to Satan for the destruction of his body that his spirit may be saved in the Day of the Lord Jesus." In other words, in this case, the man is better dead than going on living. The third case is in 1 Corinthians 11 where some people were coming to Holy Communion and were getting drunk on the wine that should have reminded them of the blood of Jesus, and were eating all the bread before the others got there. Paul says that they would become sick and die. In each of these cases there was something so horrible, so dreadful, that the Word of God says that those Christians were better physically dead. In that case, it is better not to pray for the erring brother.

I hope that has not caused you to have the wrong kind of fear; it should cause you a godly, healthy fear. That is what I understand by mortal sin because the word "mortal" here means sin that will produce death. Prayer will not be answered in that case because it is God's will to deal with it another way. But those are the only three cases, and I am not going to make a list, and not going to mention any other things which I think could be as serious. I think in the situation God will make it clear to a church that this is not the right kind of prayer for the brother, and I am content to leave it there.

The emphasis in this is on praying for the brother whose sin is not mortal, and the last word in v. 17b is that: "...there is sin that does not lead to death" – so we are to pray. When you see a brother or sister going wrong, when you see them sinning, pray for them, and God will answer the prayer and bring them back. I wonder whether you ever slipped from Christ and somebody prayed and you were brought back in. Remember what Jesus said to Simon Peter – "Simon, Simon, Satan has longed to have you, but I have prayed for you." Satan longs to have everyone. He would love to drag you back to your old life, and what will stop that happening? I will tell you: Christians praying for you.

We move to v. 18. The second thing we know and are quite sure about is that in the believer iniquity is avoided. We are up against a strong statement, which was there in 3:9, which could be misunderstood. "We know that anyone born of God does not sin." That does not mean that every Christian is perfect. Let me remind you what the verb means, using a paraphrase: "Whoever is born of God does not go on sinning." He may fall into sin but he gets up and he goes on again. He may make mistakes but he doesn't walk in those mistakes. He will pick himself up again and this is the proof that he is born of God. Indeed it is interesting that in v. 16 it says, "If anyone sees his brother sinning a sin" (i.e. a single act), but here it is saying, "Whoever is born of God doesn't go on committing sin." Why not? Because new birth leads to new behaviour.

I am thankful that Christ has a rod in one hand and a staff in the other. He is not meek and mild! Have you ever seen a picture of a shepherd in the Middle East with his shepherd's rod? It is a cosh, a great big thing; it gets fatter and fatter and there is a great wooden lump on the end. It is a useful weapon. A staff is a long pole, often with a hook on the end. You may have seen a shepherd's crook or staff. Now how does he use those two things? From time to time, out of the shadows in a deep valley, there springs a jackal or a hyena (still today in the Middle East) and it seizes on a sheep. What does the shepherd do? He puts the staff around the sheep's neck to stop it panicking and running away, and with the cudgel he beats that hyena until it goes away. The Lord is my shepherd, and as soon as the devil touches me the Lord will put the staff around me so I don't panic and run away, and he will beat and beat until Satan loses his grasp. Time and again in my ministry I have seen Satan's hold on a believer smashed by Christ. We can know that.

John now writes: "We know..." (v. 18). We have seen there is a great gulf through the human race between those who are of God and those who are of the world. The real question is: to whom do you belong? Where do you really belong in this world? Do you belong to God or the world? You can't belong to both.

You can be quite sure that you belong to God. I was thrilled when a lady told me, a week after she became a Christian, that she was "out of the rat race". She now knew that she was of God. She could see that the whole world was in the grip of an evil power and she was now out of it. To be free to rest in God's arms – what a privilege, what an honour. We are members of the royal family; we are of God; we are his children. When we look at the world we can see a world that is lying in the arms of the devil – relaxed, happy, undisturbed, and he is just doing what he wants with people.

One of my most embarrassing moments was one night when a dear girl sang a lovely song in church: "He's got the whole world in his hands." I was speaking on the text,

"The whole world lies in the power of the evil one." I am sure the girl was not singing about that. There is something of a tension or seeming contradiction here. This world of ours is in the grip of the evil one – politics is in the grip of Satan; education is in the grip of Satan; science is in the grip of Satan. If you think that is an exaggerated statement, I am prepared to back it up in detail. The whole world system to which we belong is in the grip of Satan. You can see it: every scientific discovery that has been made has been used to destroy people, and every one will. The world lies in the power of the evil one. Why is it that the UN can't bring peace? Why is it that there hasn't been a period of ten years when there has not been a major war? Why is it that we rush from one crisis to another and nobody can put things right? Can you see the whole is in chaos, in a mess. Why? Because the devil has control and he wants to destroy it. But we know that our lives are not in a mess. No, we are of God now. We are out of that rat race; we are out of that chaos. We now know where we are going. We know that we are free. Satan doesn't have the grip on us now; he doesn't have us; we don't belong to him any more. His power is broken. The whole world lies in the arms of Satan; we are in the arms of God, and underneath are the everlasting arms.

Our insight is accurate. We can know that what we know of God is real and true. You can be sure that your understanding is reliable, even if you meet a greater intellect. One of the problems of young Christians is that they meet a person who is brainier than they are, who can argue against the Bible, against Christianity, and they come and say, "Well, he really can argue better than I can." The amazing thing is that those young Christians say to me, "But I still think what I believe is true even if he's got a better intellect." You can have the greatest brain in the universe and you can be wrong about God. You can have all the education you can possibly get and you can be a fool when it comes to the things of God, but we know that our understanding is true. Our English words "real" and "true" are the same word in the Greek language. Christ really came and showed us what God is really like, and we know. Other people guess and have their ideas about God, but we know the truth. We know that the Son of God has really come and that God is real.

Therefore, we have nothing to do with the delusion of Satan. "Little children," says John, "keep yourself from idols." Why does Satan love idols? Because they give a false idea of God. They give an idea of God as an animal or a funny little fat man. Idols give a false picture of God and the devil loves you to have idols. There are three kinds of idols I know and they are all delusion. There are material idols made of wood, stone, or something else – graven images. Returning to our thoughts about the commandments, imagine for a moment that I were to say to my wife, "I love you so much that I'm going to have a statue of you made, I'm going to put the statue up by the front door, and every time I go in and out I'm going to kiss it to show you how much I love you." I know what my wife would say: "You can come into the kitchen and kiss me!" It would be such a silly way to express your love when the real person is there. God commanded us not to make any graven images. The second commandment makes sense. If you love God, you don't need a graven image, you have the real person.

There are other sources of idols. I meet a lot of people with *mental* idols. They have a false idea of God as Santa Claus or a grandfather or an insurance agent or a policeman. They have incredible ideas about God and they are all figments of their imagination. Images are imagination, and the imagination is not real and not true. Mental idols are as misleading as material ones.

Increasingly, there are also *mystical* idols: having mystical experiences, whether through drugs, meditation or repeating certain words until you have got yourself into a trance, then saying, "I've had a great experience of God or the infinite." You have had no such thing. All this is not real; it's not true. We know that our understanding is real. We know that Jesus really came, and we know that in Jesus we see what God is really like. John finishes up: "Little children, keep yourselves from idols. Amen"

Do you know that may be God's last word to mankind? We are not sure about this, but it is probable that 1 John was the last part of the New Testament to be written. I say to all who have been baptised into Christ and believe in him and know him: keep yourself from idols. What do I mean? To put it in simple English: never let anything or anyone else take the place of God in your life. If you do, it's not real, it's not true. If you stay with the God and Father of our Lord Jesus, he is real and true, and you can know that this is eternal life. So in an age when people say "I don't know, your guess is as good as mine, no-one can know", I say *we* know. We know that when we ask anything according to his will he hears us. We know that whoever is born of God does not go on sinning because Christ keeps him and the devil can't hold on. We know that we are of God and the whole world is in the grip of the power of the evil one. We know that our understanding of God is the real, true one.

2 and 3 John

2 John
A lady and her children

3 John
A man and his brethren

———

———

1–3 Love in truth
4   Following truth
5–6 Following love
7–9 Some reject truth
10–11 Don't invite them
12–13 Our joy

1   Love in truth
2–4 Following truth
5–8 Following love
9–10 Some refuse love
11–12 Don't imitate them
13–15 Your peace

TRUTH AND LOVE

Read 2 and 3 John

If you like reading other people's letters, you should really enjoy the New Testament because twenty-one out of twenty-seven books are letters. Indeed, letters are often much more revealing and much more helpful to give you insights than a prepared paper or essay. That is why in many autobiographies you tend to get "the life and letters" of so and so.

In the same way, God has seen that most of the truth that he had to give us in the New Testament came to us in the form of letters. Some of them are public, written to a whole church, but many of them are private, written to one individual. Of John's three letters the first is public but the other two are very private. They are like postcards – they are short – saying such things as "hope you are well; hoping to see you soon" – yet they are full of the truth of God, and they are most revealing. One is written to a lady and the other is written to a gentleman. I hope I won't offend anyone by saying that the second letter points up one of the temptations or weaknesses of feminine nature, and the third letter points to one of the dangers of masculine nature. That keeps the balance.

John now reveals as he writes how tender, how warm, how sympathetic a personality he is, and yet how firm he can be in relation to right and wrong. When you read back through the Gospels and discover what kind of a man he was by nature, the contrast is startling. When you first meet him he was such a bad-tempered young man that Jesus gave him a nickname, "Boanerges", which is Hebrew for "thunder".

John was revealed as one who could say: if he's not in our lot, he must be stopped doing anything. He is revealed as a scheming, ambitious man who says, "Master, when you get into your kingdom can I have the best seat?" This man becomes the apostle of love.

Quite frankly, the first thought I had when thinking about this was "There's hope for me" – and there is hope for you. If the Lord Jesus can do that with a man like that, and enable him to write letters like this, then he can do it for any of us. Human nature can be changed. My barber said to me: "Human nature can't be changed."

I replied, "That's a lie."

It is a lie of the devil actually – human nature can be changed. Thank God it can, or wouldn't heaven be miserable? Can you imagine living at close quarters forever with people as they are? But if the Lord can do this for a person and make them this kind of character and personality, then isn't heaven going to be lovely?

Both letters are about the same subject. I don't know if you spotted it. John is dealing with hospitality – the people you have in your home. This is one of the most prominent themes of the New Testament. Christians are to be given to hospitality; they are to have an ever-open door; they are to open their hearts and homes to other people. It is even a qualification to be a deacon or an elder in the New Testament. A deacon or elder who keeps his home shut to people ought not to be in office. But there are two particular needs for hospitality in the New Testament days which we don't have to quite such a degree today. Here is the first: for three hundred years they had no church buildings, and if some Christians had not opened their homes to others, the church would never have grown. If Christians had kept their front doors shut there would have been no services, no worship. Now, of course, we are in a position to erect church buildings, but we should also go on meeting in each other's homes or we shall lose a great deal.

From the very beginning, Christians did meet in larger buildings as well as their homes. They met in the temple from the day of Pentecost, every day; they met in borrowed lecture halls, and all kinds of buildings. But again and again the New Testament letters are addressed to the church that is in a house. Every Christian should be willing to open his home to fellowships and not say, "Oh well, I haven't enough chairs," or "It's too small," or, "Other people have a better home." Every Christian should say, "My home is the Lord's home for the Lord's people, given to hospitality."

They needed this in the early church not only because they had no church buildings, but also for another reason. There were two kinds of ministers in the New Testament: those who stayed put and those who moved on – and there still are. Some people are much better if they move on and some people are much better if they stay put. The pastors and teachers are better if they stay in one place and go on teaching and pastoring. The apostles, prophets and evangelists are better moving on, bringing a fresh voice and a fresh approach. So in the New Testament you have a combination of ministers who stay put and ministers who move around and that is a really healthy picture, and I hope we shall always have it.

But the ministers who move around need to stay somewhere, and in those days there were no hotels, no nice places to stay. There were inns but they were infested with vermin and disease, and were known as immoral places, and an innkeeper was little better than a pimp. So the Christian ministers didn't stay in those places. There was a real need for them to go somewhere and have a roof over their heads. Therefore 2 John and 3 John are written to Christians, describing the need to give hospitality to preachers and evangelists moving around.

Then comes the crunch. I have mentioned that 2 John was written to a lady and 3 John to a man. Here I tread very delicately, and hope to put it tactfully. Behind every act of hospitality lie two Christian principles, love and truth, and our hospitality must reflect both. Hospitality in a Christian home is not just an act of love, it is an act of truth. If you underline the two words "truth" and "love" in these two letters you find they are all the way through. "I love you in truth"; "You are following the truth"; "Follow love". Truth, love; truth, love. Love opens the door of your home and truth shuts it.

Hospitality in a Christian home must walk a knife edge between the two, knowing when to open the door in love and when to shut it in truth. Christian hospitality can be too narrow for love and too wide for truth. Our front door should be a certain width – no wider, no narrower. There are limits to Christian hospitality and we should fling our doors open right to the limit but not an inch beyond it. That may seem startling to you, so let me then elaborate it, as John does. To the lady, John is saying: your hospitality is in danger of being too wide. To the man: your hospitality is in danger of being too narrow. Speaking for the men I am quite sure he is right about the men, and ladies can speak for the ladies.

Putting it differently — ladies tend to over-emphasise love at the expense of truth, and men tend to over-emphasise truth at the expense of love. Ladies will tend to open the home to too many people; men will tend to open it to too few. That is presumably why God in his mercy arranged that a man should marry a woman and start a home together. Then they can talk about it and decide who they open to and who they close to. In other words, a lady's attitude can be too soft by allowing her heart to rule her, and a man's attitude can be too hard by allowing his head to rule him. The balance is truth and love together, and let the two things determine your hospitality. In the ladies' case, the lack of truth would lead to wrong belief. In the men's case, the lack of love would lead to wrong behaviour. Now that is simple, and God put the two letters together so we would get the balance. The reason I am taking both together is because I don't want you to think I am unbalanced one way or the other. I am neither anti-feminine nor anti-masculine; I am for them both.

Let us take the second letter. Who is the "elder" who wrote it? Many people have thought that as well as John the apostle there was some other shadowy figure called John the elder, but there is no evidence whatsoever for anybody other than John the apostle being the elder who wrote. Why did he not call himself "the apostle"? Because when a man is travelling around as a missionary, an itinerant preacher, he is an apostle; when he settles down in one place and fellowship he is an elder – which is why the apostle Peter, writing the letter of Peter to the church, says, "I am your fellow elder."

But who is this elect lady? Scholars and commentators divide a great deal over whether this is one individual, a lady and her physical children, or whether this is John's way of talking to a church. In many cases the word "you" in this letter is plural not singular, and many of the remarks seem to be addressed to a church rather than a lady. What is the answer? I think the answer is that both are right. I imagine that here is a widow who has a home, and in that home meets a church, and this lady has spiritual as well as physical children. She is one of the chosen ladies of God who has done such a lot for other people in the name of the Lord. She has a church in her house and John writes to this lady and her children.

He says this (it could be misunderstood by unbelievers, and indeed it was): "I love you." In the early days, because the Christians used the word "love" so much, there were all sorts of wild rumours about orgies and other things that unbelievers said went on in church. It was so misunderstood. People who don't know pure love have no idea what we mean by it. John says to this lady, and to the man, "I love you" and that could be misunderstood. But Jesus was a marvellous example of one who loved men and women perfectly. Those who have been transformed by Jesus can say to all men and all women, "I love you."

But you notice that it is a love in the truth. So what does that mean? Let's first look at the word "truth". *To love in truth means to love someone as they really are.* One of the reasons for getting to know each other well enough before you get married and having a period of engagement is to know each other long enough to be sure that you love each other as you are, not to have an image on a pedestal, a kind of dream that you have projected on to the other person. That will be shattered very quickly when you are living in the close quarters of marriage.

John says more than this. He says, "I love in *the* truth." Not just, "I love you in truth." Not "I love you truly" but "I love you in the truth." What does he mean? He means the truth of Christianity, the truth of Christ. To love someone in the truth means to love them as they really are as a Christian. Do you know what that means? It means you know the worst and the best about them and you love them. What is the worst that you know? The worst that you know is that the person you love is a sinner with a fallen nature like yourself and capable of any sin in the book, therefore you are never disillusioned or shattered or disappointed. You love them in the truth. It is tremendous when you can love a person like that, because the worst that you discover does not destroy your love. God loves us in the truth. He knows the worst about me, he knows the worst about you, and he still loves. He loves me in the truth; he has got no delusions about me – you may have, but he hasn't. He loves me and that is wonderful. But there is something more about a Christian. You can love an unbeliever in the truth as far as the worst goes, but now let me tell you what the best is about your fellow Christian. The best is that that person is going to be perfect; that person has Christ's Spirit in their heart and he is making them a new person. They are going to be glorified as well as justified, and you can love them in the truth for what they are going to be.

A love like that has no delusions. It believes the worst and the best. It believes the worst of what they are in themselves and the best of what they are in Christ, and one can look at a Christian and say, "I love you in the truth; I know the worst and the best about you; I know the worst of which you are capable and I know the best of which you are going to be and I love you in the truth." You can't love anybody like that outside the truth. It is the truth of Christ about a man or a woman; every one of us is capable of the most dark and terrible deeds, and every one of us believers is going to be like Christ, and you can love someone in the truth.

Apart from anything else, you know that you are not going to have to put up with their faults forever. You can look forward to the day when they are perfect in character, and they look forward to the day when you are.

When you do that, John then says that grace, mercy, and peace will be with us. How do you get grace, mercy, and peace in a fellowship of Christians? When you love each other in the truth. When you know the worst and you still love each other, and when you look to the best and love each other for it – then grace, mercy, and peace will be with you. John now says in the Greek language: *eureka*. It is translated "find" in v. 4. I can never read that without thinking of Archimedes jumping out of his bath and running down the street, with or without a towel, with great joy, excited at his discovery. John says, "Eureka, I rejoiced greatly to discover...." What? "That some of your children are following the truth." It is great when people follow the truth, when they live by reality, the truth as it is in Christ who said "I am the truth". To follow the truth is to follow Christ, and to follow Christ is to follow the truth. The nearer you get to him the more truth you will know about yourself as you are, the more truth you will know about him as he is, and therefore the more truth you know about what you are going to be.

Notice that "follow" means *behave* as well as *believe*. To follow the truth is to live it out. John calls this dear lady to follow love, keeping these two things in perfect balance. The longer I live, the more I come to the conclusion that the secret of real maturity is balance. When we are young we like to go to extremes, we like to go after one thing or another, but a mature Christian keeps love and truth in delicate and perfect balance. Love is not how you feel but how you act. It is not a matter of having great feelings of liking towards someone but a matter of doing your duty, of keeping his commandments – that is love. We must rescue the word "love" from the sentimental emotions which have now become so attached to it as almost to have excluded anything else. Let us bring "love" back to the simple matter of loyalty, the kind of loyalty that sticks to a person for better for worse, for richer for poorer, in sickness and in health, and does not let go, and cherishes to the end. In fact, it would almost be a good thing if, wherever the Bible says "love", we said "loyalty" because that is what love really is: loyalty to a person. It is not just having your heart go twice as fast as usual at the sight of someone, it is sticking by them through thick and thin. "Love divorced from duty will run riot, and duty divorced from love will starve." Those are not my words but a gem from a man called Plummer.

Now John comes to the real business of the letter. The sad fact is that not everybody in the world in which we live follows the truth. If you have children you may have been saddened how easily in their earliest years they discover that telling lies may protect them. Like every parent you will have had to correct them and say, "Now, that's not true is it?" Alas, the sad situation is that many deceivers have gone out into the world. Many people are saying things that are not true. They don't want to know the truth either about God or about themselves. They are in a state of rebellion to the truth and therefore they cunningly devise fables which are just not true. John knows that they will come to this lady and her children. He says that, above all, they will not tell you the truth about Christ.

What is the truth? We saw it in 1 John: Jesus is divine and human – perfectly one, both together—fully God, fully man. Those who are against the truth will either deny his humanity or his divinity. In John's day they denied his humanity and said he didn't really come in the flesh but was just a ghost. In our day they deny his divinity and say, "He was a great man but he wasn't God; he may have been a great teacher doing his own thing, leading people and setting them free, but he wasn't God."

There are a lot of people in the world who are telling us that Jesus is not fully God or not fully man and they will not acknowledge the truth. They may not deny it but they won't acknowledge it. I say very strongly and firmly: you must not only listen to what a preacher says, you must listen to what he does not say, because it is often in what he does not say that he goes astray from the truth.

John is telling this lady: your door must be shut absolutely tight against someone who is not there to preach the truth. That is the limit to Christian hospitality. They may be without food, they may be without a bed, you must not take pity, close the door. That is a hard thing to say. It would take grace in a woman to close the door at that point, but why should one do that? It seems such an unchristian act. The answer is twofold. A man who is not preaching the truth is doing a wicked work. John Wesley came across such a man and said, "I have met murderers of the body and I have preached to them and they have responded to grace, but these are murderers of men's souls."

It is far worse to kill a man's soul than his body. You kill his body and you are doing something that affects him only temporarily, only in this world. But if you kill his soul you have done something that destroys him forever. Therefore there are people who preach false views about Christ whom you must never have in for a meal. You must not say, "Come in," you must close the door. You must say, "There is not a welcome here." Don't even welcome him. Don't even greet him, for to say "Goodbye" to him is to say, "God be with ye."

Then John has run out of paper. He has reached the end of a small sheet of parchment, which held about three hundred words. He has so much he wants to say but is not going to put it on paper and write it in ink. He wants to come and talk this out with them. Then he says: "I want to come and see you so that my joy may be complete." Why is his joy not complete? The answer is that *some* of the children were following the truth. John rejoiced to find some of them like this but wanted to come to help all of them follow the truth, and then his joy is complete. That is the second letter of John.

We turn to 3 John. John has the same Christian love for men and women. So he says to Gaius, "I love you in the truth." In every church of which I have been minister I can think of a Gaius – a man who fits this description – and I thank God for them. His character shines out as a lovely person, yet John doesn't say, "I love you because you are lovely." He says the same here: "I love you in the truth."

Within any church, in any group, in any fellowship, there are some people you will like more than others at the human level. You are bound to. We are different in temperament, outlook and background. There are some people you take to, and if there is only liking in a church then it is not a church, it is a club. Hospitality will be too limited and homes will only be open to people of the same type, and that is not a fellowship. But when you love people in the truth you don't love them because you like them, you don't love them because they are lovely, you love them in the truth, and the truth is in every Christian. "The truth abides in us," says John, so you love everyone. John loves Gaius in the truth, the same as he loved everybody else in the truth.

Now he says, "I pray that all may go well." Sometimes I have said to a person, "Are you well?" and they have said, "Oh yes, I'm much better now, thank you." I have added, "Well, I meant more than that." To the unbeliever the phrase, "Are you well" simply means his body. If his body is well he says "Yes, I'm fine", but the Christian knows a person is more than a body, he is a soul – body and soul together. To be really well both need to be fit, healthy, and strong. The world is full of those who are well in body but desperately sick in soul. They need a surgeon; they need a drastic operation, a bad heart removed and a new one put in – a transplant, but a new heart, not a second-hand one. There they are walking about the streets; you see them, they are sick in soul. Study the faces in a London tube train next time you are taking a journey. They are well in body but you see fear, boredom, disillusionment and malice.

John says to Gaius, "I want all to be well with you." I know it is well with your soul. Isn't that terrific? There is nothing like feeling spiritually fit and healthy. It is great to feel physically fit and to be refreshed and renewed in body, but to be well with the soul...! Next time a Christian says,

"Are you well?" say, "Very well, thank you," but say it about your soul first. So John is saying: I know you are well in soul, I want you to be well in body too. A Christian can be spiritually healthy but not physically healthy. Do you notice that? There are those who believe that if everything is right spiritually everything will be right physically. It doesn't follow. Notice that John prays about physical health. It is a thing to pray about. We should pray about everything. God made our bodies as well as our souls, so we pray for the whole lot. We have a concern for the whole person. Because we believe in souls we don't neglect people's bodies, and because they have bodies we don't neglect their souls. Do you remember Paul writing to Timothy, advising him to take a little wine for his stomach's sake? Paul was concerned about Timothy's body. This was our Lord's own way. Jesus preached to a great crowd of people for three days and he met their need for some food. Concern for souls *and* bodies – this is love. Perhaps Gaius had been overdoing it. Was he tired in the Lord's service? What had gone wrong?

Now John is saying: I know that you are a man who follows the truth, and everybody else knows it. There could be few greater tributes to a man than that he follows the truth. We might say, "He's a true man, a true friend, a true Christian". It is the same thing – *true*. That is Gaius. John knows that Gaius not only follows truth, he follows love. He welcomes preachers – Christians who have left home and family and go around not for their own ambition or gain but for the Lord's sake. They refuse to take anything from the heathen so they are dependent on Christian charity.

I believe that this is a fundamental principle of the Lord's work: that his work should be financially supported by the Lord's people, otherwise it looks like commercialism. I remember when Billy Graham came to the UK, a number of people I met said, "How much is he going to get out of it?" Of course he didn't take anything for his trips to Britain so there might be no ground for anyone thinking it was commercialism.

The travelling preachers John has in mind would refuse to take any money, even if it was offered, from unbelievers. They wanted their hearers to have the gospel free. Paul did the same and I believe a church's finance should be run the same way.

Some went out for the Lord's sake and relied on him to provide for their needs through his people. Gaius was one of those who was in a position to provide for their needs.Let us make it quite certain that if one Christian lives by faith it is because another one lives by works. Do you see what I mean? If a Christian is living believing that God will provide, it is because another Christian is living as a provider. This is the pattern, and both are living by faith. One because God told them to live by gifts, and the other because God told them to give. The two become partners and sharers in the work, and Gaius was a sharer in the task. He never left his place but he shared in the missionary work. Money you give to keep a missionary somewhere else makes you a partner in mission.

Now we come to Diotrephes, who is as nasty a character as Gaius was nice. He couldn't be faulted on his teaching, his truth was alright but his love just wasn't there. He was a man who wanted to be boss of that little church. He liked to have the first place; he didn't want any rivals; he didn't want anybody else; he didn't want any other preachers. So he wouldn't acknowledge even the apostle John. He talked a lot of nonsense about him, it says. If his church members gave hospitality to a visiting preacher he took them off the membership roll. Incredible man, and he was a preacher! John makes it clear that Diotrephes is emphasising truth at the expense of love. The women were opening their doors too wide but he was shutting it too tight. He lacks love, they lack truth. Do you see the balance again? John tells them not to imitate people like that. They could imitate Demetrius, a man who was true.

I have come to the conclusion that people learn more by imitation than instruction. I don't know if that strikes you but look at your children – they imitate. The word here is, literally, mimic. That is a perfectly good way of learning.

Paul dares to say, "Imitate me as I imitate Christ." Copy those who do good not those who do evil; copy Demetrius not Diotrephes. I haven't had a Diotrephes in every church I have been in. Occasionally such thorns in the flesh come along. Learn to walk the Christian life by watching a good Christian.

John finishes the letter "Peace to you." You notice that joy in the previous letter is related to having truth, peace is related to having love. Can you imagine that church where Diotrephes was? Can you imagine their church meetings? Can you imagine the divisions? I can see them saying: "I like Cephas"; "I like Apollos"; "I like Paul," comparing ministers. You can see all that coming, and so he says, "Peace be to you." If you get love and truth in balance, you will get joy and peace in the church. If your truth is right you will have joy; if your love is right you will have peace. Isn't this lovely?

Let it be widely known in your church that your homes, church and pulpit are wide open to any servant of the gospel of Christ. Let it also be known that your homes and your church are tightly shut against those who pervert the teaching of Jesus. That is our hospitality, our Christian duty. It is a knife-edge to walk. May God give us wisdom to know where the line is and to draw it in grace and in love.

Lightning Source UK Ltd.
Milton Keynes UK
UKOW07f1126010315

247020UK00003B/4/P

9 781909 886698